His Gifts to Me

Marie Chapian

BETHANY HOUSE PUBLISHERS
MINNEAPOLIS, MINNESOTA 55438
A Division of Bethany Fellowship, Inc.

Scripture quotations are taken from the King James Version, The Amplified Bible, New American Standard Bible, New International Version, and the New King James Version. Used by permission.
Copyright © 1988
Marie Chapian
All Rights Reserved

Published by Bethany House Publishers
A Division of Bethany Fellowship, Inc.
6820 Auto Club Road, Minneapolis, Minnesota 55438

Printed in the United States of America

Library of Congress Cataloging-in-Publication Data

Chapian, Marie.
   His gifts to me / Marie Chapian.
      p.   cm. — (A Heart for God devotional ; bk. 2)
   1. Devotional calendars.   I. Title.   II. Series.
BV4811.C46   1988   88–21119
ISBN 1-55661-038-6   CIP

To Christa and Liza

Contents

Every good thing bestowed and every perfect gift is from above, coming down from the Father of lights, with whom there is no variation, or shifting shadow.

James 1:17

I ntroduction

God speaks to us continually. He speaks to us through His Word and through His servants. We can hear the voice of God in the quiet as well as the roar of life. If we listen.

This is the second book in the series called, "A Heart for God." In the first book, *His Thoughts Toward Me*, we heard the loving voice of the Savior calling us to a deeper understanding of our relationship with Him. In this volume, we hear the voice of the Father, calling us—we who are His delight and passion—into the very center of His heart.

With the same heartbeat as the first devotional in this series, we are again pursuing a closer walk with God and a deeper understanding of His thoughts toward us. His longing to be close to us far exceeds our desire for Him. The friendship He wants with His children is clearly evident in the Scriptures and the true disciple will seek such a relationship fearlessly and faithfully.

When we listen to God speak to us, we can see that through the Scriptures He has truly presented himself as wholly as our souls can grasp.

"The person who has ears, let that one hear. . . ." And so we shall.

The Scriptures show us the way to God. If we study His words, meditate upon them, act upon them, we can begin to understand our high calling as children of God in an altogether new light. Each devotion in this book shows the scripture verses to be read and meditated upon each day. As we absorb His words, His presence permeates us and we truly know we have a heart for God, a heart that only He can satisfy. Let us hear the heartbeat of the Father.

It is my prayer that His voice will supersede the human vocabulary, and I share with you again my expression of the heart of God based solely on biblical references. The breath of the Almighty gives us understanding (Job 32:8). And so, may He breathe on us as we meditate on His words—and as we receive His precious gifts to us.

Humbly,
Marie Chapian

The Gift of Concern

The Lord will perfect that which concerneth
me: thy mercy, O Lord, endureth forever.
(Ps. 138:8)

I promise you the help you need.
In My exquisite patterning
    and loving care,
I will perfect and complete all that
    concerns you.
Every particle and fiber of you
    is important to Me.
I want you to reach beyond
    your own opinions,
needs and fears;
        these hinder your discovery
    of My concerns.
I want you to stop crumbling your confidence
    into powder
with worries of survival

(calling this "concern").

Such filmy, dusty concerns keep you
  inching through life
as if you were teetering on a stony ledge
  with walls of fire on either side.
The minister of God must preach the kingdom
of God and teach only that which concerns
  the Lord Jesus Christ.
Do not preach your own concerns,
  because they won't change anybody's life
or help anyone to enter the Kingdom.
  Only that which concerns the kingdom of God
can change things.
  Only God gives life.
Fuse your concerns into Me.
  Let go and rest.
As you learn of My desires and My love,
  you will rest in My joy—
and your concerns and Mine
  will become one.

Recognize today that all your concerns
  are heard by Me.

Psalm 55:22; 1 Peter 5:7

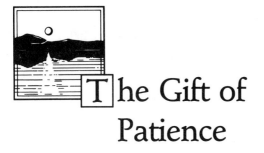

The Gift of Patience

Wait on the Lord: be of good courage, and
he shall strengthen thine heart: wait, I say,
on the Lord.

(Ps. 27:14)

You have asked me
how you can become closer to Me.
You want to know
    how to change,
        how to replace your earthly concerns
    with heavenly concerns, and how,
        when shackled at the bottom of a murky pit,
to breathe fresh air.

    Let Me tell you.
The death sentence to anxiety
is faith.
    When your anxiety overwhelms you,
fear washes a black streak

across every thought,
        and you see no end to stress, no relief.
You can pray yourself right out
        of the circle of faith.
If you could hear your daily complaints
        and grudges,
                you would pause longer
before you speak.

        Wrestle with that selfish bent
of yours,
        so quick to hurt and cry out,
                to whimper in the night,
to beg for comfort, even above your need
        for integrity.
Comfort—without My Spirit—breeds sloth
        and brings only shame.
Observe the self-indulgent people:
        They are like diamonds in the snouts of pigs,
proudly wearing their glittery gain,
        but later,
in the world's marketplace
        where I demand virtue and the holiest example,
these sparkling ones are divided like pork chops,
        swallowed and forgotten.

        Your wealth is unclean
when you cannot live without it.

Your health is unclean
when you are thankless without it.
Your accomplishments are unclean
when you think you are useless without them.
Discover daily the joy of tested faith,
the ecstasy of faith in the unseen,
and the integrity of owning nothing.

I tell you
the only way out of the murky pit
is through the top.
It is time for you to shine.
It is time to become spiritually strong;
therefore, learn the direction of the light.
You will discover the strength of My brightness
through the study of My Word
and by exercising your spirit
as My Word instructs you.
I permit many conflicts and trials
in order that your spirit
may grow strong,
in order that you shine with the glory
of an overcomer.
I will have My way: Be patient.
Do not despise the flames, My child,
but stay out of the murky pit.

Psalm 22:1–25

The Gift of Health

*Beloved, I pray that in all respects you may
prosper and be in good health, just as your
soul prospers.*

(3 John 2)

Just as the soul passes its diseases to the body,
   the body passes its illnesses to the soul.
A bodily illness may be a symptom
   of a spiritual ailment,
and a disease of the soul may be a symptom
   of a physical ailment.
Rather than castigate your soul too swiftly
   when you are ill,
      rushing backward toward guilt and
      worrisome confusion,
   consider your nutrition,
      your bodily health.

Are your mind and body

starved for better care?
Your nervous system, bones, vascular system,
    hormones, muscles, glands and vital organs,
intricately designed to serve you,
    require your attention.
The divinely appointed functions
    must be cared for
because they can each play a part in
    spiritual depression.

Show your godly sanity
        today
by caring for your body
    with utmost seriousness.
Every cell, tissue and nerve has been formed
    to be strings for My fingers
        to play upon,
    creating harmony and energy
in order that you may be
    strong and of good courage.
Today, enter the solemn business
    of being at your best—
    body, soul and spirit—
        for Me.

1 Thessalonians 5:23; 1 Corinthians 15:44; 6:18–20;
Jeremiah 30:17a

The Gift of Wholeness

*But Jesus turned him about, and when he
saw her, he said, Daughter, be of good
comfort; thy faith hath made thee whole.*
(Matt. 9:22a)

I created you as a total person.
    If you are sick in one part
    you pass on that sickness to other parts.

Your entire person must be redeemed:
    I provide total redemption for all of you;
    I provide cleansing for your mind,
        so consumed with fears and worries;
    I provide forgiveness
        for the devastating choices you've made,
        willingly sinning against yourself
        and Me;
    I provide peace
        to penetrate your emotions,

tattered by the cares of life
and worn by lack of visits to Me
for your daily supplies;
I provide health for your body—
more than enough to make of you
a good and valiant servant!

It is My will that your entire person
express praises to My Name.
It is My will that you count your body as precious,
that you do not compare yourself to others,
nor be threatened by years or infirmities,
but that your mind be solidly fixed on Me,
whole,
and full of My salvation.
You are not a partial person—
not even if you believe it to be true.

Colossians 2:10; Philippians 4:13; 1 Corinthians 15:49; 2
Corinthians 3:5; Proverbs 17:14; 1 Timothy 6:20; Isaiah
55:7; Philippians 2:5; Romans 8:11

The Gift of the Left Cheek

. . . whoever slaps you on your right cheek,
turn to him the other also.

(Matt. 5:39)

Stop blaming the environment for your problems.
  Stop blaming heredity.
  Stop blaming others.
  Touch your left cheek for a moment.
  Is it smooth, unscarred, unblemished?

How is it that a child of Mine
  should have a smooth, unbruised "other" cheek?
Can you tell me that?

  My clearly stated word to you
  is to rise above the pain of life
  and turn the other cheek
  for more!

Understand the meaning of this admonition.

If you grit your teeth and bear an insult
bravely,

you turn only the right cheek.
But I have told you to ascend, intensify,

strengthen, progress and prosper

by turning your left cheek, too.
You cannot turn

your left cheek
after being slapped on the right

without supernatural confidence
in what is already yours.

Confidence does not grit its teeth

unless it's already lost.

When you are full of Me—
full to *overflowing*,

rich in My grace and abilities,

you suffer no real disgrace or poverty.
Nothing can be taken from you
if you do not possess it.

And that is why

you willingly

turn your left cheek.

Human blows cannot weaken

what you have and are in Me.

Romans 8:13; Galatians 5:24; Philippians 3:8; Matthew
5:11–16

The Gift of the Second Mile

And whoever shall force you to go one mile,
go with him two.

(Matt. 5:41)

You are never so weary
    that you cannot go the second mile,
never so humble,
    that you cannot bend lower;
never so bereft
    that you have nothing left
        to give.

        I give you *abundant life,*
        and that means more and more—unending!
True, overcoming faith
does not scrape the edges of the bowl,
does not grapple, beg
or cajole for favors.
        Faith does not scramble for bites of life,

nor hide from earthly blows.
The child of God has strength
for one more mile.
The first one was for man,
the second one is for Me.

Hebrews 12:3, 12–13

The Gift of Mercy

You have heard that it was said, "An eye for an eye and a tooth for a tooth." But I tell you not to resist an evil person. But whoever slaps you on your right cheek, turn the other to him also.

(Matt. 5:39)

If a brother or sister wrongs you,
consider it a slap to your right cheek.
But if you refuse to bow to anger
and resentment,
and choose to do *good*
to the one who wronged you,
you have presented your other cheek
and won a surpassing victory.
You are *more* than a conqueror.
More.

My ways are always *more*

Abundant.
Full to overflowing.
Great and exceeding.
Ever-increasing.

Have you been insulted, rejected,
unjustly accused?
My Son was called a gluttonous man,
a simpleton, a drunk
and a fraud.
My servants have been called
cannibals and rebels;
they've been sold as slaves,
raped and sawn in pieces.
My Son has demonstrated
holy, perfect power,
the capacity of My heart and soul,
by not demanding His human rights,
not seeking to save his life,
and my servants can know this conquering power.
The world asks only for your right cheek
and you may give it grudgingly,
but I demand the left as well.
Then you will shine, as with
precious stones
fit for a King's crown,

because you know
there is no loss on earth so great
that I am not greater still.

Romans 8:31–39; 13:10; John 12:25

The Gift of More

Yet amid all these things we are more than conquerors.

(Rom. 8:37)

To increase in Me,
you must decrease.
Do not settle for less from yourself,
    than learning to turn the other cheek,
    and to walk the second mile.
Do not accept giving only what is convenient.
Do not permit yourself to stand still
    in a muddy spray of
        anger and self-righteousness.

I know you.
If I know you and love you
    and if I am for you,
        who can be against you?

A conqueror is far more than one who endures
with sliding eyes and bitter heart.
A conqueror accepts the blow to the right cheek
and is glad for the opportunity
to turn the left cheek,
which I alone can see.
Begin to think
more.

Romans 8:31

The Gift of Opportunity

If there is among you a poor man, one of
your kinsmen in any of the towns of your
land which the Lord your God gives you,
you shall not harden your [mind and]
heart, or close your hand to your poor
brother; but you shall open your hand
wide to him, and shalt surely lend him
sufficient for his need, which he lacks.
Beware lest there be a base thought in your
[mind and] heart.

(Deut. 15:7–9a)

The greater the pressure on you,
　　the greater the opportunity
for the law of the Holy Spirit
　　to be exercised in you.

Suppose you are taken to court,
　　you're accused and slandered

and everything you own
(except your bed)
is demanded of you.
I tell you: Do not war in your mind.
Seize the opportunity:
Give all (and offer the bed as a bonus).

And what about those who ask favors of you—
who plead with you for money,
send you pathetic letters
and pound on your door for help
when you ache to rest?
I tell you, do not grumble in your heart.
Seize the opportunity:
Give to those who ask
and if you can hear these words,
give so the one receiving
gets your maximum best
in kindness and divine regard.
If you do not restore integrity
to the poor,
if you do not respect and honor
every soul in distress and need
as you would a ruling prince,
you have not heard Me clearly.
You have not understood.

It is not only

goods or money
I require of you;
Not only your brotherly deeds,
kind acts
or enviable leadership.
I want you to give far more than is
expected of you.

I want you to embrace the stony hearts
so chipped and marred by sin's disease
and love them for me.
If your enemies are unreasonable,
nasty-mouthed and tyrannical,
do you fight back, defend your pride
and growl yourself to sleep at night?
Or do you take the opportunity
to gladly give kindness, wisdom and mercy
like a flowing river, sweet and easy?

When in the call of duty,
do you give the irreducible minimum
and not one breath more?
If you are efficient and punctual,
gracious, but determined to do only your job,
nothing more, nothing less,
you have not opened the gift
of opportunity I've often sent.
Yet My heart is not troubled
and I'll never turn My face away

while you selfishly pursue your own gain,
>in My Name.
So I'll send you opportunities
>and opportunities
and greater will be the pressure on you.
>For if I am kind to ungrateful and evil persons,
then you will be, too.
>You will be merciful
>>as your heavenly Father is merciful.
The opportunity
is now.

Matthew 5:40, 42; Luke 6:35–36

The Gift of the Human Will

For that which I am doing, I do not understand;
for I am not practicing what I would like to do,
but I am doing the very thing I hate. But if I do
the very thing I do not wish to do, I agree with
the Law, confessing that it is good.

(Rom. 7:15–16)

Victory is not found in your human will.
I have shown you by the words of my servant Paul
    that even though you *will* to do good,
        your will is not forceful enough
    for the tasks you confront and defy.
So you sink, shamefacedly, to the deeds
    and behaviors you hate.
        To *will* is with you,
            but to *do* is not.

In the flesh of humankind,
    the law of sin is served.
And though you delight in the law of God,

you need a higher law
        to overcome a lower law.
You need the law of the Spirit of Christ
        to conquer the law of sin.
Your human will, in itself,
        cannot conquer the law of sin.
The law of the Spirit of life in Christ Jesus
makes you free from the law of sin and death.

I have already won your personal struggle
                against sin and misery,
                        and I have set you free
                to live happily and with self-respect.
        I have condemned
        that which would condemn you.
                I give you the free gifts
                of life and sanity
                        in exchange for your gift
        of a willing human will.
I ordained, at the beginning,
        that your will would become
                a priceless, golden instrument
                        for the Holy Spirit to master
                                and to make one with My will.
        That is your perfect victory
                and your power.

Romans 7:22–23; 8:1–3; 6:22–23; 8:9–17

The Gift of Strength

For to me to live is Christ, and to die is
gain.

(Phil. 1:21)

You have asked that I empower you
to be a person of strength
    and courage,
and I hear you
        and I want to answer.
But there is something missing with you.
    I empower the beloved and priceless souls
who live and breathe with the new life I give,
    who know and believe in the risen Christ
and who boldly exclaim to an uncaring world:
    "For me to live is Christ!"
    They show the Way, the only Way
to receive strength and courage.
    If you would be strong and courageous,
you must exchange *you* for *Me*:

35

My life for your life;
   My Holy Spirit for your human weakness.

Do you think of Me
as an occasional beneficent visitor?
   A distant, kindly relative?
Or do you think of your holy heavenly Father
   as you would an addition on a house?
      —an improvement to
         an already existing structure?
I am your life.
   I'll have nothing less
      than your life from you.
   You live *now*
      if My Son, Jesus Christ,
         lives in you *now*
by your assent and belief in His atoning love
   and sacrifice.
      He is your Advocate and Friend.
   Through Him I can breathe thoughts and words
      into your mind and being.
         You will hear Me
            and My words will become alive
      within you.
My Spirit will connect and infuse,
   creating Him in you.

Listen.

I speak to you now.

Be strong and of good courage, I tell you.

Strength is in you.

Galatians 2:20; 2 Corinthians 13:4; Romans 8:11; John 14:17; 1 Corinthians 6:17; John 1:12–14; 11:25; Deuteronomy 31:6

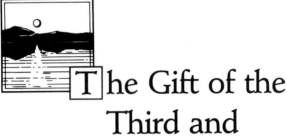

The Gift of the Third and Fourth Mile

If your enemy is hungry, give him food to eat; and if he is thirsty, give him water to drink.

(Prov. 25:21)

I want you to understand the "extra mile"
    that I require of you.
        Can you see the road ahead?
If so, you have not gone far enough.
If you are still able to stand,
    you have not walked long enough.
If you still have a piece of bread in your bag,
    you haven't relinquished enough.
If you still have a coat and a bedroll,
    you have not offered enough.
When will you see that
    My grace is more than bare sufficiency?

You lack nothing.

You want, expect, pray and plead with Me
    to give abundantly,
        to bestow material blessings upon you.
    But when do you give to Me?
You present Me with skimpy little tokens:
here and there a kindly deed, sporadic prayers,
    favors with a frown,
        a rare and reluctant tear
            for someone other than yourself,
    a gentle gesture in the presence of others;
        noble words of advice
            you do not follow yourself.

I long to receive something genuine from you,
    your third and fourth mile,
which are your most exquisite gifts to Me.
I am not requiring you to seek punishment,
    denials and sufferings.
    That is the way of false religions;
those rites which lead poor, hungry souls
    astray are designed to teach the
        emptying of self.
But I do not want you empty.
        I want you filled with Me!
I formed you to be sweetly,
    triumphantly

and totally
full of the divine Spirit of Christ.
And then you are at peace with the extra mile,
which I will always place before you.
No matter how many times
you run in the other direction,
no matter how often
you moan and groan that it's too far,
I will never remove the extra mile.
You may now stop blaming life
and others
for the road you must travel—
It's our road
and we travel it together.

Philippians 1:11; Romans 8:18; 2 Corinthians 4:17; 9:8;
Isaiah 66:2; Luke 14:11; 18:18–20; Matthew 25:23

The Gift of Transcendence

This day the Lord thy God hath commanded
thee to do these statutes and judgments:
thou shalt therefore keep and do them with
all thine heart, and with all thy soul.
(Deut. 26:16)

Why are My commandments so strict?
Why are My assignments
    impossible to perform?
Do you think I ask too much of you?

I hear your shifting, deadly, stunted thoughts.
I hear you conjecturing the ways your God is rigid,
      narrow-minded, unyielding,
hard-nosed, unfair.
    Shall I say more?

I am these things
    and more

if you choose to think so.

My commandments are more strict
    than those of human origin
    because I want it said of you
that to know the strength of your love
    requires being your fiercest enemy.
    I want it said of you
that no sorrow can exceed your joy,
    no ill treatment can surpass your capacity
for mercy,
no physical hardship can limit your service to Me,
    no tragedy of life can empty you of hope,
no disparaging vision can alter the Truth
    engraved in your heart.

You see, Beloved, I know
that by receiving the spiritual presence
    of My life and mind,
you are empowered to know and live in truth.
    I know
you cannot transcend the cares of life
    alone,
and you cannot fulfill My commandments
    alone.
    Nobody can.
I command you far beyond your human potential.
    I command you to go the extra mile

when you don't want to.

    I command you to call on abilities you do not have
        in your human power.

    Give your human limitations daily
to be possessed, *empowered* by the indwelling
        presence of My Spirit.

    Have I not promised,
        You shall receive power
        when the Holy Spirit has come upon you?

    His indwelling power
transcends your inabilities
and fulfills My commandments.

You will *love* one another as I love you,
    you will *accomplish* all that is yours,
        You will *keep my Word*, hide it in your heart,
purpose to obey it
    and have good success;
    and you will *go the extra mile*,
with understanding and contentment in your soul.

    You cannot begin to fulfill My commandments
without My Holy Spirit.

    This is the life you were called to live
at the dawn of your journey with Me.

    You are never stretched too far,
        because for you to live is Christ.
In Him there is no exhaustion,
    no frustration,

no complaint,
no anxiety or fear.
Your life is already finished.
It belongs to Me.

Romans 8:6, 26, 28; 10:8–11; Joshua 1:8; 2 Corinthians 4:17–18; Acts 1:8; John 2:3–5; Ezekiel 36:27; Colossians 3:3

The Gift of Feeling Good

*But if the Spirit of Him who raised Jesus
from the dead dwells in you, He who raised
Christ Jesus from the dead will also give life
to your mortal bodies through His Spirit
who indwells you.*

(Rom. 8:11)

Look at the way you react to situations:
    For example, you view sickness
as an opportunity to rest.
    You tell others you are ill
because God is trying to get your attention.
    What nonsense!
        How quickly you ascribe the cares of the world
to the hand of God,
as if I find pleasure in your pain
    and happiness in the affliction of My children.
        You comfort yourself falsely
for I am not pleased to see you

sick and ineffective.
Am I like an insect
    on a perfect rose,
a disorderly germ in an orderly world?

I am the Lord of glory!
    I reign over all;
in My hand is power and might
    and I give strength to all.
No thought is withheld from Me.
    With Me all things are possible.
    I appointed the foundations of the earth.
By My Word the heavens were made,
    and all their host by the breath of My mouth.
I love righteousness and justice;
    the earth is full of My lovingkindness.

I observe intently all the inhabitants of the earth
    from My dwelling place
and My eye is upon My own beloved children
    to deliver them from the devourer
and to keep them alive in times of lack.
    Those who trust Me shall be compassed
about with mercy and lovingkindness.
    I have no pleasure in wickedness,
but I answer the righteous one's cry for help.
    I deliver from distress and trouble;
        I am close to those who are of a broken heart,

who are without harmony and peace.
I heal, save and deliver my children from many evils,
including their own foolish, evil thoughts.

Bring to Me the disharmony of your life
that I may bring melody
and perfect order to you.
Give Me your unrest, your unhealth,
that I might restore balance to your spirit,
soul, and body.
Surrender your false thinking regarding illness.
Your body is an instrument for My purposes.
I desire your attention when you are fit and well,
not only when you're ill.
Is your body worn like a used, thread-bare coat,
unable to resist disease?
Give Me your fatigue, your weary bones, and
I will give you My rest and strength.
I want to quicken your mortal body.
Today, I want to see you strong.

1 Chronicles 29:12; Job 42:2; Matthew 19:26; Proverbs
8:29b; Psalm 33:5–6, 18–19; 32:10; 6:4a; 34:17–19;
Matthew 11:28; Romans 8:11

The Gift of Creativity

And he shall be like a tree planted by the
rivers of water, that bringeth forth his fruit
in his season; his leaf also shall not wither;
and whatsoever he doeth shall prosper.

(Ps. 1:3)

Creativity does not mean the same as
      originality.
      Only I am original.

The *measure of life* you bring to your world
      is the measure of your creativity.
            Do not approach a task as a dead person
            with dull, vacant eyes
            staring at shapes and movement
      as though all things are the same,
            your good deeds like skittering mice.
The secret of your creativity

is how you view taking up your cross
   and following Me.
Hungry, selfish eyes never see creatively!
   They have a cunning, crafty view,
disturbed by pride and need,
   but such eyes never fully see what really is,
because the view is stumped and dwarfed,
   unilluminated.

   I am the Creator,
and in Me you lose yourself
   and your limited interpretations.
So deny yourself,
   disown fleshly visions,
   refuse a stilted, worldly view
and take your blessed cross
   which keeps you close to Me
      where all creativity resides.
   I bring light to your mind,
I refresh your energies,
   I bring you to your truest, holy self.

Originality is not
   doing something no one else has ever done,
   but doing what has been done countless times
with new life, new breath,
   as only you can bring.

How painstakingly the artist trains her hand
to record the world around her;
how long and arduous are the hours the
musician
practices to form the sounds notated on the
paper;
and how endless is the writer's task
to record in words the language of the heart.
Yet all belongs to God.
All is, and all was,
and all will be Mine.

Do not bond with your own soul.
Bond with Mine.

Luke 9:23–25; John 15:5

The Gift of Discovery

For if you cry for discernment,
Lift your voice for understanding;
If you seek her as silver,
And search for her as for hidden treasures;
Then you will discern the fear of the Lord,
And discover the knowledge of God.

(Prov. 2:3–5)

Discover knowledge and discretion.
They are pleasant to the soul.

They watch over you,
keep you, deliver you from evil people.

When you discover skillful and godly Wisdom,
more precious than rubies,

you will learn that nothing you can wish for
can be compared to her.

The discovery of wisdom will be
life
to your inner self,

and a gracious ornament to your neck
 for all to see.

Wisdom reveals confidence and trust.
 Wisdom teaches you not to be afraid,
  contentious, jealous, or unscrupulous.
Wisdom founded the earth,
 understanding established the heavens.
  Length of days is in her right hand,
and in her left hand are riches and honor.

 Discover the tree of life
and lean on, trust and be confident
  in Me.
  I am the giver of all things.

When you panic over the small loss
  of one hair on your head,
 or when you panic at the great loss
  of health and home,
you knit your heart to scorn and unbelief.
 I have said, "Lose your life—all of it—for Me."
If you save, cling to and treasure
your own precious well-being
 more than the discovery of wisdom and truth,
you lose the very thing you long for.
 You resort to pinched, crabbed glimpses
 of what you *wish* were beautiful and lasting.

Discover Me afresh each day
in wisdom, holiness and humility
and I'll declare you blessed;
I will make you joyful,
favored with abundance,
and you shall inherit glory,
all honor and good
and a new identity.
Stop your lonely pleas
to stubborn, unyielding strangers;
end your sleepless, aching nights,
with mornings more dark than midnight.
In such a life you are all your own
and none of Mine;
in such a life
you are not a work of art at all,
but a mockery of what
you were born to be
and possess
and discover.
What profit do you have when you gain the whole
world
but you have no *self*?

Proverbs 3:15, 22, 23, 26, 30, 31, 19, 16, 5, 33b, 34;
Luke 9:24; Proverbs 3:35; Matthew 16:26

The Gift of Responsibility

Be not wise in your own eyes; reverently
fear and worship the Lord, and turn
[entirely] away from evil. It shall be health
to your nerves and sinews, and marrow
and moistening to your bones.

(Prov. 3:7–8)

You are not responsible for the body
with which you came into this earth,
but you are fully in charge
of the one you bring to Me now.
How much has your body been influenced by fear,
worry, doubt, anger,
anxiety, hatred, bitterness?
I did not send My Son to die only for your soul,
For I have redeemed you—
spirit, soul *and* body.
I want to allow My blessings
to engulf your entire being.

If your body functions with limitations,
I love even that which does not function wholly,
because I love *you* wholly.
But do not allow bodily limitations
to limit Me in you.
You are whole,
not because your body is whole,
but because I am whole.
I give you My wholeness
in order that your entire self
will be filled with Me.
To open your inner self, your spirit, to Me
is your responsibility.
My wholeness and tender love
is perfect in your disabilities
as well as in your abilities;
I am perfect in your health
and in your unhealth.

Only your mind can cripple you.
Your body's pain can deeply affect your mind,
but, oh! my dearest, I am ever present in your pain
to deliver you from the sins of complaining,
fear and anger.
My Son suffered physically, too,
and He died a bloody, painful death,
because He trusted Me and knew
He had to give Himself for you.

You desperately need to take His life,
    each moment, hour and day
to mold yourself into Me,
    to become responsible for the discovery
and maintenance of My divine
    relief, exquisite joy and inner health,
        that no human mind or body
    can duplicate.

Matthew 11:29

The Gift of Multiplication

Now for this very reason also, applying all diligence, in your faith supply moral excellence, and in your moral excellence, knowledge; and in your knowledge, self-control, and in your self-control, perseverance, and in your perseverance, godliness; and in your godliness, brotherly kindness, and in your brotherly kindness, love. For if these qualities are yours and are increasing. . . .

(2 Pet. 1:5–8a)

My Spirit multiplies
    everything of Myself in you.
When you walk in the way of insight
    and understanding,
you choose My wisdom,
    which multiplies with use.
Hear instruction and be wise

and do not refuse or neglect My words.
Listen to Me and be blessed.

   Allow Me to fill your treasuries,
for My increase is better
than the world's choice silver,
   and the fruit of the Holy Spirit within you
is better than refined gold.

   Good gives birth to good, multiplying itself.
I give you the gift
   to multiply the good you already have.
   You will forever draw forth
and obtain favor of the Lord
   when wisdom builds your house.
Wisdom comforts you when your increase slacks;
   she feeds you with the Bread of Life
and gives you spiritual tonic to drink,
   to delight your soul and revive your spirit.
And as your wisdom is increased,
   your understanding multiplies.
Your godly thoughts,
   your self-control, perseverance,
      kindness and love
         multiply,
and your soul delights itself in fatness.

   I grant you precious and magnificent promises
so you will become a partaker of My divine nature.

As you take of My kindness,
    kindness multiplies in you;
as you take of My compassion,
    compassion multiplies in you;
as you take of My forgiveness and mercy,
    forgiveness and mercy are multiplied in you;
as your faith accepts My righteousness,
    which atones, makes clean and reconciles,
My righteousness
    becomes yours.
You are
    one with Me
        and I will multiply *you*.

Proverbs 9:6; 8:33; 8:19; 8:35; 9:1, 5; Isaiah 55:13, 3;
Romans 3:22, 25

The Gift of Anointing

For we are a fragrance of Christ to God
among those who are being saved and
among those who are perishing.
(2 Cor. 2:15)

I send you because you and I
are bonded together in My Spirit.
　　You care as I have shown you I care:
your arms are now My arms,
　　embracing the forgotten and neglected;
your smile is now My smile,
　　enveloping the anxious and depressed;
your hands are now My hands,
　　helping the weak and helpless;
your voice is now My voice,
　　bringing hope and life to the cowardly and dying.

You are like a sweet perfume to those
　　who have made their beds in garbage heaps;

you are a carrier of blessed light
     to those who are without sight;
you carry with you the healing balm of compassion,
     which heals the wounds of mind and body;
your ears are not deafened to the cries
     of despair and agony.
     You have time,
because you and I are bonded together
     in My Spirit;
no distance is too far for you to travel
     to bring a lost and dishonorable soul to Me;
no river too raging,
          no mountain too ragged
as you climb the crags and search the pits
     for those who have lost their souls
as they tried to gain the world.

     Brace up your heart, My beloved one;
set your face like a flint, and listen:
     Do you hear the children calling, crying?
     Do you hear the hungry clamor
          of the rejected and despised?
     Do you feel the plight of the poor
          and the one who is crushed in spirit?

     Go ye into all the world.
Your platform may be an airplane, a bus, a park bench,

kitchen table, coliseum, TV studio, radio microphone,
book, baseball field, desert road, lakeside,
campground, refugee camp, foxhole or deathbed.
I tell you,
Go.

Luke 9:1–6

The Gift of Serving

*Whoever speaks, let him [or her] speak, as
it were, the utterances of God; whoever
serves, let him [or her] do so as by the
strength which God supplies; so that in all
things God may be glorified through Jesus
Christ, to whom belongs the glory and
dominion forever and ever. Amen.*

(1 Pet. 4:11)

This is your finest hour.
This is the hour you have studied,
    prayed
        and worked toward.
    I have prepared you,
and you have been My faithful student and servant;
    you have done well.
Enter into My inner courts
    where My Son has prepared a place for you—
enter into and share the joy and blessedness

of your Lord!
My Son has revealed and taught you
    all that He learned from Me
and it gives Him great gladness
    to present you to Me as His friend.
I tell you these things
    so that My perfect joy
        and delight,
    the personality of heaven,
        may be ingrained in you,
and that your joy and gladness
    may surpass human emotion,
be full in measure, complete and overflowing,
    because you live in Me
    and I live in you.

Confidently be about your Father's business
to find the renegade, the prodigal, the lame,
    to love the unlovable and the fearsome,
        to kiss the wounds of the battle-worn,
    to lift up the weary hands which hang down,
        to wash the calloused, aching feet,
        and to win the lost.

Beloved, bring My children
    home to Me.

Matthew 25:23; John 15:15, 11, 4

The Gift of Abundant Labor

Therefore, my beloved brethren, [and sisters] be steadfast, immovable, always abounding in the work of the Lord, knowing that your toil is not in vain in the Lord.

(1 Cor. 15:58)

I will hold you up, My beloved,
when your precious foot slips;
    so never curse the stones,
and certainly not your foot.
    I will help you when you hurt,
I'll bring songs of joy to your ear
    when you're sad,
and words of encouragement
    when you're unsettled.
I'll breathe peace into your worried heart;

I'll quiet your restless thoughts.
And I'll forgive.
    I'll forgive.

You are My ambassador
    to the world I've put you in;
You represent the King of kings.
    You speak My words
        and make known My thoughts.
Be firm, steadfast,
    immovable, abounding
    in My work.
Dare to do more than required,
    exceed what is expected,
        because you love your labor,
knowing the highest calling in My Kingdom
    is to be the slave of all.

Proverbs 3:23; Isaiah 53:5; Zephaniah 3:17; Psalm 29:11;
34:18; Acts 3:19; 2 Corinthians 5:20

The Gift of God's Presence

My presence shall go with you, and I will
give you rest.

(Ex. 33:14)

You have many doubts and fears.
    I am with you
to shed light into every dark, disturbed area
    of your mind.
I assure you continually
    that I am with you;
I have not forsaken you.
        I am ever faithful to you
and I am there for every need you have.

        I seek out the dusty corners of your mind
where strange images lurk,
    and where battles have raged,
leaving wreckage and festering sores.
    But I am Lord of your personal psychology;

I am Lord of your past and your future;
I am Lord of your conscious and unconscious;
I am, my dear one, Lord of all that concerns you.

I want you to discover
the fullness of joy
in My presence;
I want you to discover
beauty for ashes;
I want you to learn that in My presence
you can break every yoke of bondage
that has held you captive
and you can take My supernatural power,
which I freely give,
to walk by faith, not by sight
and to be controlled by Love
and wisdom.

No interior battle is too fierce
to confront head-on, full-faced,
when you're wearing your armor.
The hidden enemy you fear,
the one who seeks to destroy your life in Me,
must face Me before he reaches you.

Because you have chosen to be
transformed by the renewing of your mind,
and because you come daily to Me,

as one alive from the dead
and an instrument of righteousness,
it is time for you to become at peace
with My presence.
Take the oil of gladness
instead of mourning;
take the covering of praise
instead of tiring introspection.
Renew, refresh, rekindle
and guard the sound mind I have given you.
In place of fear and timidity,
meditate on these things
in My presence.

Isaiah 61:3; 2 Corinthians 5:7, 14; Romans 12:2; 6:13;
Ephesians 6:11; 1 Timothy 4:15

The Gift of Confidence

*Let us therefore draw near with confidence
to the throne of grace, that we may receive
mercy and may find grace to help in time of
need.*

(Heb. 4:16)

Your arms are filled with bundles of
    needs and wants.
Your back is bent with a crushing load
    of cares and fears.
Your face is stiff with grim anticipation
    of desolate tomorrows.
This is how I watch you drawing near.
        How much mercy and grace
        will you require of Me
        once you get here?
Your mind is not on mercy as
    your heart races
and you pant with exhaustion,

climbing my holy mountain,
drawing nearer. . . .

I watch you pause to rest
and to reconsider the petitions
    you would present to Me.
    You worry briefly:
"Will He hear me?
Will He answer?"
        My throne seems so far away,
        and such a great climb to reach it.
You're convinced that you're weak
    and insignificant
and that the cares of life have overwhelmed you.

I have given you a Savior
who sympathizes with your weaknesses.
    He triumphed, sinless, over temptation
so you could triumph with Him.
    Draw near,
        draw near, I say.
Not with chin drooping and mouth pouting.
    I am here on the throne,
        watching you approach;
        I am waiting
        and I want to see the confidence
    of My Son in you
        boldly shining,

boldly knowing
I *am* Mercy.

Nothing concerning you is hidden from My sight.
All things are open and laid bare to Me.
Bring Me your burdens with confidence;
bring Me your troubles, trials and pains
with confidence in My holy power.

Asking without confidence
is like a gift without a giver.

Hebrews 4:14–16; 6:14

The Gift of Sleep

When thou liest down, thou shalt not be
afraid: yea, thou shalt lie down, and thy
sleep shall be sweet.

(Prov. 3:24)

I give My children perfect slumber—
yet nightmares invade your sleeping hours
and you awaken agitated,
spent,
unrested.

I am Ruler of all heaven and earth,
I am your Creator,
I am your Provider,
your Safety,
and when I look upon your face,
My heart exults with tenderness.
For you have joined yourself to My Son;
you are one in Spirit with Him

73

and your body has become a temple—
    yes, a lovely, luxurious temple
for My Spirit to maintain in perfect holy order,
    for My Holy Spirit to saturate
    and dominate so entirely
that you are not your own,
    but a glory to Me.

I will not in any way fail you,
    nor give you up.
I will not leave you without support.
    I will not
        will not
        will not leave you helpless.
            I will never forsake you,
            or
            loose My hold on you.
I reside in the temple of you,
    and I am passionately forming you
        in the image of My perfect Son.
I give you sleep that is sweet,
    like nectar,
refreshing and invigorating.

    Give Me your sins and fears
    and allow your body to sink softly into My arms,
where no thieves will break in and chase you wildly
    through mountain, plain and city deserts;

where no oceanic tidal waves will roar above you,
    eager to overwhelm and crush you;
where no gulping, fetid swamps of mud
    can swallow you whole;
where no scheming devils steal your loved ones
    and your goods;
where no curtain rises on a stage
    where you stand frantic
    with no script or score;
where no car you drive suddenly races
    uncontrollably
        without brakes;
where you do not lose your teeth,
    and snakes do not coil around you,
    and nobody murders you.

Oh, My child, come to Me now,
    let Me hold you,
        soothe you,
            sing to you
    and release you
    from your fear of silence.
Come, My child,
    do not be afraid of peace,
        for the night was not meant
        to accomplish the work and cares of the day.
    Give yourself

to Me,
     and sleep.

Psalm 3:5; 4:8; 1 Corinthians 3:16; Hebrews 13:5;
Romans 6:17; 19–20; Psalm 42:8b; Exodus 33:14;
Jeremiah 31:26

The Gift of Security

Now to Him who is able to keep you from
stumbling, and to make you stand in the presence
of His glory blameless with great joy. . . .
(Jude 24)

Lean your entire human personality
on Me.
    Trust
that I am loving,
    good, and just.

You ask why I permit evil
    to exist,
and why I allow My godly ones
    to suffer.
        I tell you,
        evil, wherever it is found,
    bears within itself,
        the seeds of its own destruction.
Evil, if wrought by evil people

or by My own children,
will destroy itself.
　　Only in My righteousness is there power
　　　　to withstand and persevere;
　　only in My holiness can you stand erect
　　and immovable.
Apart from Me you can do nothing:
　　It is Law.
And the Law of the Lord is perfect,
　　restoring the whole person,
　　　　making wise the simple,
　　　　　　rejoicing the heart,
　　　　　　　　enlightening the eyes.

Bind My words, My law, to your heart,
　　speak them aloud, tie them
around your neck as a
　　golden leash.
And when you walk about,
　　My words will guide you,
and when you sleep
　　they will watch over you
to make sweet your dreams
　　and keep you safe from harm.
And when you are awake
　　My words and I are alive
in you and your mind is illuminated,
　　　　ignited by holy wisdom and truth
and you are no longer confused.

Because you know the word of My power
    I watch over you.
        I am the shade at your right hand:
    The sun will not harm you by day,
        nor the moon by night.
    I keep you from all harm,
        I watch over your life;
    I watch over your coming and going
        both now and forevermore.

My bountiful free gift to you is
eternal life through My Son, Jesus.
Human understanding fails to comprehend
    this gift,
    so I ask you to give Me your human
understanding
    that I might set fire to it—
    create sizzling, crackling
        flames of truth within you.
    You see, dear one,
you are secure,
    not so much because you understand,
but because
    I say so.

Psalm 118:5–6; John 15:5; Psalm 19:7–8; 121:5–8;
Proverbs 6:20–21; Romans 6:23; Jeremiah 23:29; Psalm
119:89

The Gift of
Knowledge

*The mind of the intelligent seeks
knowledge, but the mouth of fools feeds
on folly.*

(Prov. 15:14)

One small seed is the birthplace
    of a mighty forest;
all creation was born
    in a sole holy thought.
Just so, knowledge spawns knowledge.

    My children acquire knowledge,
      store up knowledge,
and wear knowledge as a crown
    because knowledge begins
    with Me:
      I am Knowledge.
Recognize, be aware of and *know*
    the One who daily pleads your cause

to Me,
   the One who defends and instructs you
is your most holy Lord and Savior.
   To Him I have given all glory,
      honor, majesty
   and perfect knowledge.
Know Him and you will gain Knowledge
   impenetrable.
Be knitted to Him, Who is your royal Advocate;
   He gathers you
in His compassionate thoughts
   to melt the ice of fear and unholy ignorance
and to breathe the fire of knowledge
   into the shivering crevices
   of your soul.

Proverbs 18:15; 10:14; 14:18

The Gift of Knocking

Behold, I stand at the door and knock; if
anyone hears My voice and opens the door,
I will come in to him, and will dine with
him, and he with Me.

(Rev. 3:20)

My children are weak and silly with lack of
knowledge.
    Their eyes dart across the skin of life
seeing only surfaces and edges,
    but not within or underneath.
They are captivated by actors wearing heroes' masks,
    intrigued by beguiling, deadly, dancing snakes,
        and they classify and give names to things
to love or hate or be indifferent to.
    They measure worth
        by comparing one shallow surface
            with another.
They are like doors,

shut tight and dumb;
like rutted and ancient brass doors,
　　　　with hinges nailed.

Who will press against the pale outer edges
　　of these barricades
and allow Knowledge to come in?
Who will knock upon the door?
　　Lift up your head, O my child,
　　　　and lift up the entrance of your mind to truth.
　　For I shatter ancient gates of bronze,
　　　　I break the battered doors of tradition
　　and cut the bars of ignorance asunder.
　　　　Naivete is enmity with Me.
I am the King of Glory,
　　and I stand at the
door and knock at this moment.

　　If you will dare to open and learn of Me,
there will be revealed to you a place of wisdom,
　　established in understanding
and filled with treasure.
　　You will discover the *new beyond,*
where My Spirit reveals
　　the hidden wealth of heaven's secrets.
My children must learn
　　that their hungry eyes

have never truly seen nor understood
what their God has prepared for the ones
who knock.

Psalm 24:7–10; 107:16; Isaiah 45:3; 1 Corinthians 2:9

The Gift of Prosperity

Then you shall prosper, if you are careful to
observe the statutes and the ordinances
which the Lord commanded Moses
concerning Israel. Be strong and
courageous, do not fear nor be dismayed.
(1 Chron. 22:13)

I'll teach you how to prosper,
and I'll lead you in the way
    you should go.
Your well-being will be like
    a clear flowing river,
and your righteousness like the waves
    of the sea.
I'll make your offspring as grains of sand
       and they will never be cut off
from My presence.

But when your neck is as iron sinew

and your forehead stubborn bronze,
when spells and sorceries whistle
melodies from a defiled mind
    lulling you senseless and stupid,
when you lie corrupted by astrologers
    who babble empty prophecies by stars and moons,
when you play your life
    as on a game board
choosing personalities from a hat
    in search of your hidden self,
when you manage your business
    as on a gambling table,
when you seek flattery
    and are quick to chase fantasies,
        you become as a twittering crane,
            a moaning dove, a seeker of luck
            and your prayers are noisy;
    the songs you sing are not the ones
you learned from Me.

    Where is the faithful child
who loved to learn of Me,
        who diligently obeyed
    and communed with Me?

    Will you languish, dusty-eyed,
        and crusty at the mouth,
            until you become vinegar to the teeth

and smoke to the eyes?
I tell you the hour is here
    to take up your cross and follow Me
        and you will prosper again.

Isaiah 48:17–19; 48:4; 47:12; 38:14; Proverbs 10:26

.

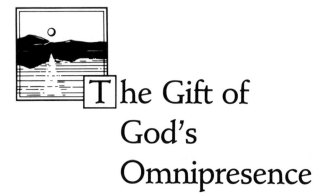

The Gift of God's Omnipresence

"Am I a God who is near," declares the Lord, "and not a God far off? Can a person hide himself in hiding places, so I do not see him?" declares the Lord. "Do I not fill the heavens and the earth?" declares the Lord.
(Jer. 23:23–24)

I have searched you and known you,
    I know when you sit down and when you rise up,
I understand your thoughts from any distance,
    I scrutinize the choices you make
        and I am with you
            when you lie down to sleep.
I am intimately acquainted with all your ways.
Even before you utter a word, I know it.
    I have enclosed you with My protection and love
        from before and behind.

My hand is upon you always.

So I ask you:
Where can you go from My Spirit?
Where can you run from My presence?
If you try to scale a ladder to heaven,
I am there;
If you take a backpack trip to hell,
I'll be there;
If you climb upon the wings of the morning
on an early flight to the ends of the earth,
or if you book passage on a ship and live in its belly
in the center of the sea,
My hand will be there to help you.
My right hand is able to protect you
and hold you close.

O dearest one, with storm-tossed thoughts,
think on this:
My mind is in your mind.
My Spirit is over your spirit.
My *self* is in yourself.
My presence is in your presence.
For I saw you before you could be seen,
and I wrote about you
when there was nothing to write about.
My thoughts of you outnumber the sands.

The speed of light cannot outrun Me,
darkness and light are alike to Me.
Neither by night nor day
can you escape My heart.
You cannot be unloved.

Psalm 139

The Gift of Acceptance

When my father and mother forsake me,
then the Lord will take me up.
(Ps. 27:10)

When your anxious thoughts multiply
    like mosquitoes in the grass
—when your foot skitters faster than an arrow
    over slate
—when you shout for help in a vacuum of silence,
I will always come to you.
I will deliver you,
    rescue, honor and satisfy you
because you love Me
        and your fears and doubts
    are swallowed in My lovingkindness.

You are in the light
    as I am in the light,
though you may sometimes forget.

I have called you to be
as a burning sun in My Kingdom,
    shining brightly, boldly,
and a joy to those whose lives you touch.

    Yet you are without honor at home.
Should you take offense?
    Should I?
Should you forbid to bring assistance
    to the ones who are your enemies by day,
but at night plead for your mercy and your help?
    Should you not feed the hungry
when they eat now and throw stones at you later?
    Should you turn away from the sick,
    because they do not believe in Me?

When the world around you rejects you,
    rejoice that I accept you wholly.
For the world does not know Me
    and they mock and care for themselves
as clouds without water, carried along by winds.
    If your enemies are as autumn trees,
    barren and fruitless,
    you keep yourself in My love.
Build up your most holy faith,
    pray in the Holy Spirit,
because I have not called you
                    as a heavenly war chief

to snuff out the naughty ways of My lost children,
　　though they reject you
and scorn you as wild waves of the sea,
　　casting their shame like foam
on everything they touch.
　　I ask you to accept them.

Dearest, the light will always shine in darkness
　　regardless whether or not
the darkness comprehends.
　　You are boldly shining,
from your residence
　　in the tabernacle of My heart.
But they make their beds on burning coals.
　　Who will snatch them from the fire?
Who will accept and show them to the Door?
　　Will you?

Psalm 94:17–19; 91:14–15; 1 John 1:7; Matthew 13:43,
57; 1 John 3:1–2; Jude 12–13; Revelation 3:20; 1 John
1:5; Psalm 27:4–5

The Gift of Courage

Be strong, and let your heart take courage,
all you who hope in the Lord.

(Ps. 31:24)

I have examined you
　　and I have tried you.
I have also heard you in your affliction
　　and your loneliness;
I have observed when the troubles
　　of your heart have been enlarged
and distress has covered you.

　　But I am the guardian of your soul
and I deliver you from self-defeat.

　　I give you integrity and uprightness
to preserve your spirit,

　　Did you know that?

Courage dwells
　　in the integrity of your faith,

for I vindicate the righteous;
    I am your light and your salvation;
I am your ability to be courageous
    and I am your capacity to be courageous.

The extra mile I assign you
    can only be approached
        with a stout and enduring heart.
And as you are brave and of good courage
    you can be sure you will succeed,
        for I guide you with My truth
and My strong right arm.
    I lead, instruct, and help you along each path
        I set your feet upon.
All My paths are paved with mercy,
    and each drop of sweat that falls from your brow
        is met by My cooling grace;
    each step you take in pain is cushioned
            by My billowing grace.
    I do not call your name to bring you weariness,
    nor do I desire to rob your zeal
        with harsh demands.
        Oh, My dear one,
    toilsome though the extra mile may be,
        the joy of the journey will be great,
    because I have given you the secret
        of My sweet, satisfying companionship
    and I delight in encouraging you.

As we go hand-in-hand,
  heart-in-heart,
      I-in-you and you-in-Me,
I will continually reveal to you
  from faith to faith,
      precept upon precept,
the deep inner meaning
  of your prayer
      for courage.

Psalm 26:2; 25:16–18, 21; 27:1, 14; 25:5; 2 Corinthians
12:9; Psalm 25:14

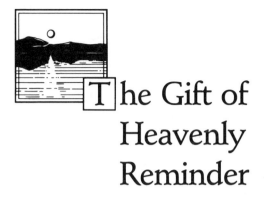

The Gift of Heavenly Reminder

Therefore, I shall always be ready to remind you of these things, even though you already know them, and have been established in the truth which is present with you.

(2 Pet. 1:12)

Have I wrung out the clouds with My fists
and hung them to dry like rags in the wind
    that you should look up and despair?
Have I forgotten to command the morning,
    or cause the dawn to know its place
that you should find fault with Me
    and contend with Me?

        Do I not make the clouds My chariot?
        Do I not walk upon the wings of the wind?
        Do I not also make flaming fires

of My ministers?
Yet you dispute with Me.

Will you condemn your God
    that you may appear righteous and justified?
Was it you who established the earth
      upon its foundation?
Is it your voice that is heard
      upon the waters?
Are you the God of glorious thunders?
    Is your voice powerful, full of majesty
    breaking the cedars,
    splitting and flashing forth forked lightning?
Tell Me, by what is light distributed,
    and how is the east wind spread over the earth?
Has the rain a father?
    Who has begotten the drops of dew?
Can you gather the chains of Pleiades,
    or loose the cords of Orion's constellation?
      Can you?
And do you know who determined the
    measurement of the earth?
Was it you?
      Tell Me if you know.
Have you an arm like God?
    Since you question My rule,
    show Me your majesty and
    array yourself with excellency and dignity

befitting the supreme God.
Demonstrate your holy honor
and glory and wisdom
by undertaking the government of the world.

If you can do all this,
    proving yourself of divine might,
then I, God of All There Is,
    Maker of heaven and earth,
will praise you
    and acknowledge that you,
        a created human being,
            justly bear a claim against Me.

If you do not dare arouse
    the wild beast to play with him,
do you dare contend with Me,
    the beast's Creator?
Everything under the heavens is Mine,
    and yet you contend
        with Me.

Psalm 104:3–5; 29:3–5; Job 38:25, 28; 40:9–10, 14; 41:34

The Gift of
Sustenance

*Cast your burden upon the Lord, and He
will sustain you; He will never allow the
righteous to be shaken.*

(Ps. 55:22)

You wring your hands and chew your lip
as your bills mount up
    like the spikes of spired shrines.
You rush back and forth in panic,
    complaining to those who cannot help,
like an exhausted swimmer
    alone on a troubled, endless sea.

In My goodness I provide for the needy.
    I am He who defends the cause of the poor.
Is it that, in your riches,
    you do not consider yourself poor?
In whatever state you're in,
    I am your Provider

and your Protector.
Why, then, do you fret?

Do not be ashamed of your utter helplessness.
Place your whole trust in Me:
This pleases Me.
"Blessed are the poor in spirit,
for theirs is the kingdom
of heaven."
Is it that, in your religiosity,
you do not consider yourself poor in spirit?
Do you wish the Kingdom of Heaven
to be at your disposal
free of charge?

Precious child,
I would be far more pleased
if your heart would be at peace
than to hear your momentary sighs of relief
when your prayers are answered.
I owe no man,
so detach yourself from worry
and take My sustenance.
The removal of your debts and troubles
will not bring you joy,
but perfect trust and peace in Me
is great gain.
Without My peace you will chafe

and agonize
again and again
over troubles large and small.
And when you do,
you will be oh so certain
that you're once more swimming helplessly
in blackened enemy waters
bereft and alone
but
you
are
not.

Psalm 68:10; Matthew 5:3; Philippians 4:11; John 14:27;
Psalm 29:11

The Gift of Life

And this is eternal life, that they may know
Thee, the only true God, and Jesus Christ
whom Thou hast sent.

(John 17:3)

Am I difficult?
Is following Me so burdensome?
The flesh blanches and rebels
    at My directions,
but the flesh is not eternal—
    it withers and dies.
        I do not.

Do you bow your knee to the law
    of sin and death,
or do you celebrate the law of *life*
    in Christ Jesus?
        Which is it?
If you will take the gift of life,
    which I freely give,
you will love being a new person.

Old fears and troubles
will no longer be a noose around your neck;
you'll marvel and behold
that all things have become new!
I give My unmerited grace—
not for self-administered consolation
or self-appointed absolution.
(These won't last; they have not life.)

You find Me difficult
when you find no comfort
in My words.
You do not realize
you are laboring falsely
to keep some part of your life
under your own control.
Self-interests blind you,
deafen you,
stiffen your joints
and fatten your neck;
too much knowledge can prove
your ignorance.

When your heart is broken,
you blame Me.
Will you not pull yourself
from worldly attachments
which only lead to sorrow?

Will you not come out
    from your billet in the shadows,
where you commiserate by the hour
    with other hungry souls
        who are as desperate
as you are?

    As the dawn returns, bright and new,
each day,
    so new life
waits for you.

Romans 8:2; Revelation 22:17; 2 Corinthians 5:17; 2
Peter 3:9; Proverbs 8:35

The Gift of Godliness

Discipline yourself for the purpose of godliness.

(1 Tim. 4:7)

Consider yourself in training:
Every day you must exercise
    for spiritual fitness.
As the love of Christ controls,
    urges and impels you,
you will take one step
    at a time.
You will learn how to walk by faith
    and not by sight.
    Then, swift and smooth,
you will be running,
    not on blistered hopes
and groaning, aching schemes for a better life;
    but you will aim yourself,
sure and steady,

on a straight course,
preparing for the race
that has already
been won for you.
The tutoring of My Spirit
is not simply to prepare you
for the contests of the human will,
nor for the uncertain rewards
of your labor.
Spiritual discipline in godliness
extends to all things pertaining to you
for both time and eternity.
Godliness has the seed of itself within;
it multiplies with use,
changing your entire outward life.

The life of God revealed in you
becomes your crown and glory,
and Mine, too.

Philippians 3:12–14; 1 Corinthians 9:24–25;
1 Timothy 4:7–8

The Gift of
Holiness

But like the Holy One who called you, be
holy yourselves also in all your behavior;
because it is written, "You shall be holy,
for I am holy."

(1 Pet. 1:15–16)

Your tears,
which soak the shoulder of God,
   are like jewels He keeps
in His holy box.

I am He who pardons you,
dries your cheeks and lifts
   the burden of sin
      from your back.
I am He who hears you when you sigh,
   and catches you when you fall.
Once you were burdened
   with a heavy load of sin,

and then you came to Me.
   And now as a child of God,
you appear to be burdened
   with a heavy load of holiness.
I have never asked you
   to live a holy life in your own strength.
How can you, being human,
   call the majesty of holiness
into existence?
      How can mere dust
live a creative, powerful life
   in wisdom and authority
      (not to mention love)?
Dust has no life of its own,
   but just one breath from Me
and dust became a human race.
   Can the clay command the potter?
Can the dust rise up and will itself alive?
   Not by might,
   not by power,
   but by My Spirit, I say.

Oh, it pleases Me when you
   live in harmony with My Spirit;
your gifts to Me
         of discipline,
   obedience,
profitable, godly exercise

and love for Me
are as fragrant aromas.
    In your sacrifice,
you grow to radiate the heart of God
    in bright rings of holiness
and peace at last.

    You are holy as I am holy,
because I have made the dust
    to live.
    Your heart will sing "Alive! Alive!"
Not you,
    but I in you.
    Your burden of holiness is not heavy
because I carry it for you.

Colossians 2:13; Jude 24; 1 John 1:9; Luke 1:74–75;
Ezekiel 36:27; Genesis 2:7; Romans 9:20; Zechariah 4:6

The Gift of the Cross

And after He had appeared in human form
He abased and humbled Himself [still
further] and carried His obedience to the
extreme of death, even the death of [the]
cross!

(Phil. 2:8)

I want to open the eyes of your understanding
so that you can see yourself as you really are:

When you came to Me
    your sins,
sensuality and carnal nature
    had you fastened to death
like a fly caught in a spider's web,
    making motion but going nowhere;
but today, because you are mine,
    your sins, your carnal nature,
with its passions and lusts,

are stripped from you
and nailed to the cross of My Son,
      Jesus.

When I created you, I had in mind a *friend*.
    The path to My friendship
is by way of the cross of Christ,
    where your sins are nailed
—where your old life is buried
    with Christ
and your new life is raised
    with Christ.
He did the dying for you.
    Your sins are no longer in you
    but on the cross.
And so it is with your personality,
    wants, needs and goals;
they, too, are there,
    on the cross.
    When you ask for forgiveness,
I am faithful to forgive your sins;
    so when you fear that the power of sin
      may defeat you,
don't look at *you*;
    look at the *cross*!
There you will see yourself as you really are—
    your old self on the cross,
      crucified with Christ.

Your real self lives through Him,
    and daily you are renewed and remolded
after the image and likeness of Me.

    Do not reject your cross.
        It is your gift.

1 Corinthians 1:17–18; Colossians 2:11–15; 3:10;
Galatians 2:20

The Gift of Godly Plans

"For I know the plans I have for you,"
declares the Lord, "plans to prosper you
and not to harm you, plans to give you
hope and a future."

(Jer. 29:11)

Call upon Me today and I will listen.
Seek Me with all your heart because I am yours.
As surely
    as I made the heavens
to be a tent for the sun,
    I will keep you.
I will cover you with My shadow,
    and protect you under My pinions.
As surely
    as the anthem of the stars
and the voice of the moon
    are heard through all the earth,
singing the message of My glory,

so shall I sing over you.

When you strain and grunt laboriously
    in efforts to remold yourself
and your world,
    you weary yourself.
Neither a bird nor a wolf
    can act like a Christian;
and neither can you do the work of God
    without Me.
I tell you to find your life in Me,
    to live only by My Spirit—
but not by striving,
    nor by anxiously reciting old prayers
like charms,
    nor by agonized self-recriminations,
nor by works or
    hammering at the heavens
with preposterous offers and deals.

    Listen to the words of My instruction,
    for I have a plan for you;
study to show yourself approved,
    for I have a plan for you;
apply your heart to what I teach,
    for I have a plan for you;
increase your knowledge of Me,
    for I have a plan for you;

gain spiritual discernment and wisdom,
    for I have a plan for you;
take My yoke upon you and learn of Me,
    for I have a plan for you;
give up hope in yourself for trust in Me,
for I have a plan for you
        today.

Jeremiah 29:12–14a; Psalm 19:4b; 91:1, 4; 19:1, 4; John
20:21; Proverbs 8:33; 2 Timothy 2:15; Proverbs 1:5

The Gift of Armor

Put on the full armor of God, that you may
be able to stand firm against the schemes of
the devil.

(Eph. 6:11)

Your worst temptation may not be
the stirring to sin,
    but rather attempting to resist sin
without your spiritual armor.

Your enemy, the devil, entices you to sin,
and what is worse,
    he stirs
        your old nature into action.
If you can be tempted to resist temptation
    with your own strategies,
you are easily conquered.
    Self-will can never stand before
mighty spiritual controls.

The real enemies of humankind are not
other humans,
    but powers and master spirits
who are the world rulers,
    the spirit forces of wickedness.

My holy armor is truth, integrity,
    moral rectitude,
        right standing with Me
    and firm-footed stability.
My holy armor is a shield
    of incorruptible faith in Me,
    with My Son, Jesus, held high over all.
My holy armor is your hope
    of surmounting every difficulty,
and your protection
    as you defeat every enemy
through the blood of the Lamb.
    My holy armor is My written Word,
a mighty sword
    that cuts to pieces
every snare of the enemy.
    My holy armor will defeat the temptation
and the tempter,
    so you must put on every bit of it.
Then you will stand firmly.

Defeat is not caused by less effort

on your part,
but by too much effort
without protection.
Today,
put on your armor.

Ephesians 6:11–17

The Gift of Joy

This day is holy to the Lord your God; do
not mourn or weep. . . . Go, eat of the fat,
drink of the sweet, and send portions to
him who has nothing prepared. . . . Do not
be grieved, for the joy of the Lord is your
strength.

(Neh. 8:9b–10)

My love for you insists
    I give to you
the best of Me,
    the joy of Me.
The walls of heaven
    are assembled in such joy.
Their whispers go out continually
    on the wings of the wind
of eternity:
    I am joy!

I rejoice over you
    and I delight over you.

I want to prosper and multiply you
     so you will do good.
I faithfully watch over you
     with all My heart and soul
as you build and develop
     in all the areas of your life.
The gift of My joy
     is consummate,
unassailable,
     relentless,
quintessential.
          No person can take it from you;
          no change of life or circumstance
               can alter,
                    diminish
               or remove My joy from you.
I give you joy as a vital spark
     that sets fire to melancholy
     and self-protection,
that burns to dust
     discontent and the fear of loss.
          I give you joy
               that seeks and finds you
          in the midst of pain and sorrow.
Joy calls your name,
     pursues you,
          stretches forth her arms to you.
Joy is hungry to embrace you so tightly

that no worldly pollution
can seep through her broad back
to dampen a single one of your thoughts.

Deuteronomy 30:9; 28:63; Jeremiah 31:28b, 41; John
16:22; Isaiah 51:11

The Gift of Delight

He brought me forth also into a broad place;
He rescued me, because He delighted in me.
(Ps. 18:19)

Because you place complete trust and confidence
in My character and will,
    you will never be disappointed.
Because your hands are clean
    and you have lived in conscious integrity
    with a sincere heart,
        I multiply My gifts to you.

        I delight in you.
You are kept perfectly in the secret place
    of My love and holiness,
        where bitterness and rancor are far from you.
You savor with gladness all of My ways,
    and the exquisite peace of My joy
        is yours.

When Love creates your path,
>> your path becomes blameless,
for your God loves righteousness.
> Because you have shown yourself kind,
I will show My kindness to you.
> Because you have shown yourself merciful,
I will show My mercy to you.
> Because you have shown yourself pure,
I will make all things pure to you.
>> I delight in you.

> Your unswerving faith in my character and ability
>> keeps you safe
and you will not be overtaken by your enemies.
> You will crush a troop of evildoers;
>> in My strength and prowess
you'll jump high walls and stand securely
>> on dangerous heights of testing and trouble.
I train you,
> protect you,
>> uphold you
—not by raging force,
> for it is not My might and power
>> that makes you great,
> and grants you passage
>> to ride upon the high places of the earth,
but My gentleness.

I have proved your heart,
and I have found pleasure
in joining your delight
with Mine.

Psalm 18:19–35; Isaiah 58:14; Psalm 17:3

The Gift of the Morning

The Lord's lovingkindnesses indeed never
cease, for His compassions never fail. They
are new every morning.
(Lam. 3:22–23a)

Come to Me
in the morning.
    Think of My strength
and My lovingkindness.
    For I have been your stronghold
in the hours of your soul's darkness,
    and I have been your protection
in the blackness of every distress.

Oh, in the morning
I love to hear your voice
    as you lift your prayer to Me,
and I love your eager heart
    waiting for My voice.

For morning by morning
    I awaken your ear to listen
in order that hope will burst forth in you
    with the vibrant colors
        of the dawn,
and that your righteousness will march before you
    with the glory of the Lord
as your rear guard.

    I have heard your weeping in the night hours,
when your tears were the only distinction
    between you and the dead.
I tell you, fear paralyzes
    and renders my children lifeless,
    as though the eyelids of the dawn
were those of a monster
    out of whose mouth spew dangers
more searing than fire.

    Meet the morning with a smile of gladness,
        My beloved child.
For surely if you listen to the voice of the sunrise,
    you will hear her shouts of joy!
You will hear the anthems of My mercies
    and lovingkindness,
and you will be enjoined
    to the hosts of My holy family
who daily offer themselves willingly

in splendor and holy array.
Then from the womb of each morning
  the beauty of worship is born anew.
Beloved, I want you there.

Psalm 59:16; 5:3; Isaiah 50:4b; 58:8; Psalm 30:5; 65:8;
110:3

The Gift of Laughter

Blessed are you who weep now, for you
shall laugh.

(Luke 6:21b)

Laughter does not exclude weeping.
When pain and hardship confront you,
    and the scars of oppression line your face,
I will remove the sting of defeat
    and the burning sensation of failure
and loss.
    Joy is no stranger to pain.
When you sow in tears,
    you will reap with sounds of joy
coming from your mouth.
    When you go out from your interior pain,
weeping, but carrying the seeds of hope
    to plant in spiritually barren deserts,
you will return one day
    accompanied by joy and laughter.

I am faithful to burst forth life
from tiny seeds.
I *am* Joy.

Do not be common, dull of hearing
and full of ignorance.
Gladness and laughter are not attained
by eliminating pain and suffering.
Joy is not an escape from sorrow,
like a drug.
Rather, My joy gives power to rise above sorrow
in all situations.
My knowledge is within you,
giving light to the words,
"No eye has seen, no ear has heard,
no mind has conceived
what God has prepared
for those who love him."
And this is why
you are confident and free in your heart
to toss your head
and sweetly laugh.
Your laughter is My gift to you;
as it tumbles upon my ears
like the sound of many glad waters,
it tells Me that you,
My darling one,

have learned the private language
    of heaven.

Luke 6:21; Psalm 126:5–6; 1 Corinthians 2:9; Revelation
1:15

The Gift of a Joyful Noise

Make a joyful noise unto God, all the earth.
(Ps. 66:1)

Your laughter is without derisiveness and scorn,
because you do not run from pain.
    You can rejoice in the midst of your discomforts,
not only bearing injustice and dishonor,
    but exalting in triumph.
Blessed hilarity accompanies you
    as you emerge from your self-imposed captivity.
You pinch your thigh and wonder,
    is your happy heart a dream?
        It is not.

I have filled your mouth with laughter
and your tongue with joyful shouting,
    for there is a time to weep,
but also a time to laugh.
    Laughter is a friend of grief and suffering,

and only the vain and
    self-protecting soul recoils from it.
If you pursue pleasure instead of joy,
    you win pleasure's thin reward.
I remind you of the cost of joy
    and laughter:
It costs your tears,
    your wandering mind,
        your sorrows
            and your shame.
Rejoice with Me,
    again and again;
never pause to sigh or click your teeth at hardship,
    because I rejoice eternally
and together our laughter
    can fill the world.

Psalm 126:2; Ecclesiastes 3:4; Philippians 4:4; Isaiah
35:10; Psalm 89:15

The Gift of the Sound of Joy

But let all those who take refuge and put
their trust in You rejoice; let them ever sing
and shout for joy, because You make a
covering over them and defend them; let
those also who love Your name be joyful in
You and be in high spirits.

(Ps. 5:11)

The sound of joy
    is like the stretching of trees,
reaching upward
    to brush the floor of God.
The sound of joy
    aspires higher than a human utterance,
resounding from one corner of the earth
    to the other,
so exhilarating
    it awakens that which lies in waste.
Joy startles the parched riverbeds,

it stirs the dormant desert
and prods the slumbering hills
     so they meet in gladness,
clapping their hands
     to the roar of the sea in its basin.
The sound of joy
     is like that of a host of celebrants
marching in triumph
     to the house of the Lord—
and even the rocks follow,
     singing.
The sound of joy
     is like that of the mountains
shouting their mysteries across
     the generations.
The sound of joy
     cries out as a voice in the wilderness,
exulting and proclaiming
     the glory and majesty of God.

Let everything that has breath
     and every breath of life
hear the sound of joy,
     for God walks in its corridors
and kisses the hearts of His children
     who glory in His greatness.
Sing songs of triumph
     with the hail, the fog and the frost,

for in the choruses of the rushing wind,
  and within the swirling
heights and depths of the sound of joy,
  you will hear
the voice
  of the heart of God.

Psalm 98:6, 8; 100:1; 150:1–6

The Gift of Stillness

Meditate in your heart upon your bed, and
be still.

(Ps. 4:4)

The ship I give you has no rends or tears
     in its sails.
  Its pilots are Wisdom and Truth.
The names of the crew are:
    Integrity,
       Honesty,
          Prudence
             and Contentment.
Though the course may become choppy
    as storms of greed, pride
       and desire for comforts
    lash at your vessel,
you will not be lashed apart.
      I am Captain.
    I won't abandon you

and I'll not allow your ship to sink.
I won't steer you in circles.
    There is no need to be
        threatened or anguished.
    Trust in the wisdom of your pilot.
Take the hand that guides you daily
    and be still.

The storm you face is not in the waters;
    the storm is in your ship—
within you.

    Let the wind in your mind no longer roar;
let your wicked heart,
    troubled and turbulent, rest.
To your raging thoughts
        I say, "Be still."
    To your fearful, troubled imaginations
        I say, "Be silent."
Before you speak adversely and
    in confusion,
        I say, "Be quiet."
In the stillness of your heart,
        I speak to you.
    You will hear a gentle voice,
softly
softly
        infusing you with new strength
and faith

to understand My ways
and know the sweet composure
of a quiet heart
even in the storm.

Mark 4:39–40

The Gift of Victory

But thanks be to God, who gives us the
victory through our Lord Jesus Christ.
(1 Cor. 15:57)

You are victorious
because you choose to be.
Faith's experience builds the
palaces of victory,
and the builders
are your thoughts.
I created you to live
in the palace of victory.

I have visited you
with My courage,
and I am not weak toward you,
but mighty *in you*.
My Son was crucified
because of human weakness,

and He goes on living
by My power
in you.

Within your house of victory
My strength and power
are made perfect,
fulfilled and completed—
not in your human strengths, but in your
human weaknesses.
If you would live as a shadow,
leaving no footprints on your world,
giving nothing of value,
nothing of heaven,
then
continue to carry the knives of fear
in your thoughts.
Your mind is your enemy and your defeat,
not the world around you.

I have told you to put on the armor of light,
for through My Spirit,
you will overcome inordinate anxieties,
and in My name you will tread them under
who rise up against you—
the howling voices,
whining fretfully in the night,
these enemies of your mind,

clattering through your noons and sunsets,
spreading chaos and turmoil.

Your victory will be your glory
when you give your efforts fully to Me,
    for I willingly share My victory
        with you.
    I am in dominion over all;
the heavens and the earth are mine.
    In My hand is power and might;
right there, in the center of My palm,
    lies your greatness
    and your strength.

Today
    choose victory.

2 Corinthians 13:3–4; 12:9–10; Romans 13:12; Psalm
44:5; 1 Chronicles 29:10–12

The Gift of Restoration

Then you will say on that day,
"I will give thanks to Thee, O Lord;
For although Thou wast angry with me,
Thine anger is turned away,
And Thou dost comfort me."

(Isa. 12:1)

I comfort you,
    comfort you.
And in My kindness,
    I call out to the heart of you
to tell you that your warfare
    will be ended
        and your iniquity removed.
For though you have polluted your calling
    and sinned against innocence,
I am calling you
    to clear a path through the emptiness
        of your life.

Make a smooth path from your heart
       to your mind
that the Lord might return
    and take residence upon the throne
        of your soul
once more.

Isaiah 40:1–3

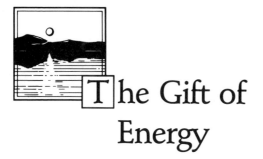

The Gift of Energy

Do you not know? Have you not heard?
The Everlasting God, the Lord, the Creator
of
the ends of the earth
Does not become weary or tired.

(Isa. 40:28)

Because My understanding is infinite,
    unsearchable,
        inscrutable,
because My love is life
    and holy energy
forever,
    I heal your broken heart
and bind up your wounds
    when you cry out to Me.

There are no outcasts in My kingdom,
    no weary, beleaguered, undone,

145

pathetic pariahs
  for whom the angels jeer or sob.
I count the stars and give names to each of them;
  I count the tears
on your chin, My beloved one.
  My eye is on you when your foot is slow.
Love is strength,
  and I am able to support you;
I open the palms of My hands
  to make a path
for your slow foot to run upon with ease.

  I bring the wicked to their knees
in the garbage heaps of their pursuits.
  I am He who does not restrain lightning
from striking My adversaries;
  I breathe into the sky
so that clouds and rain are formed;
  I create snow like wool
and command it to shroud the earth;
  I scatter frost like ashes
and I say to the downpour of rain,
  "Be steady."
How can the natural abilities of the thing created
  stand securely before the everlasting Creator?
What pleasure have I in the strength of a horse,
  or the capable legs of a human being?

I am searching for the weak,
    the weary;
for to the person who lacks might
    I increase power.
I give strength to the weary.
    I energize.
When you trust in My strength
    to accomplish your many activities
and to overcome your many trials,
    you will gain new strength;
you will mount up with wings like eagles.
My strength empowers
    the legs of My chosen ones
to run and not grow tired,
    to walk and not become weary.

Young lions,
    though they are strong,
become hungry and weak;
    they have no voice to cry out
in prayer to their God for help,
    and it is not to them
I give My power and energy,
    but to *you*, My own,
to you.

Psalm 147:3–5; Romans 11:33; Job 37:2–7; Isaiah 40:28–
31; Psalm 34:10

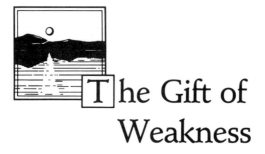

The Gift of Weakness

He gives strength to the weary,
And to him who lacks might
He increases power.

(Isa. 40:29)

It is a good thing to recognize your weakness.

It is a good thing to cry out, "Who will help me?"
I am the LORD your God who says to you,

Do not fear, I will help you.

I am He who created the heavens
and stretched them out;
I am He who spread out the earth
and all that is upon it;
I am He who gives breath to the people of the earth
and spirit to all who walk upon it.
I will hold your hand and watch over you;
your emotions will not defeat you
and you shall not be swallowed by your failures.

Even when you feel forsaken,
desolate and feeble of heart,
   I will find pleasure in you.

   Learn to extract the precious
from the worthless,
   and you will become as My own mouth.
I am with you to save you
   and deliver you from depression
and anxious thoughts,
   for I have made you weak
not to become as the weak,
      but wise,
   a gift from My holy, loving heart
that you might become strong-hearted
   in Me.

Isaiah 41:14; 42:5, 6b; 62:4; Jeremiah 16:19–20

The Gift of the Narrow Gate

*Enter by the narrow gate; for the gate is
wide, and the way is broad that leads to
destruction, and many are those who enter
by it. For the gate is small, and the way is
narrow that leads to life, and few are those
who find it.*

(Matt. 7:13–14)

There is an easier way to live
than the way you have chosen.
There is a cheerier road to travel,
strewn with confection, comfort,
auspicious work and agreeable friends—
and the entrance gate is
wide.
You can travel this road,
that is, if you don't mind waiting
in line
among the hoards of others

who have chosen to enter the wide gate, too.
　　The waiting area at that gate
has walls papered with
　　brightly colored promises,
and vendors sell endearing romance stories
　　written on loaves of bread
that the people eat,
　　and when they belch, they don't know why.
There are shops where dying souls
　　promote their eternal health products,
while bent and broken men and women
　　run madly throughout the throngs,
　　　　begging for donations,
　　political favors
and a ride in your car.
　　There's a gum you can chew
guaranteed to bring you luck on the stock market.
　　There are temperaments
you can pick from a hat
　　if you want to marry right, lose weight
　　　　or do well in graduate school.
Life is a party, say the people
　　who choose the wide gate and the wide road;
　　　　it's self-centered, cruel and vain,
　　and God is not invited there.
So when the lights finally go out
　　and the party is over,

nobody goes home,
    because there are no homes
        along the wide road
that leads to destruction.

    This is why I tell you
to choose the narrow gate,
    the one you must shrink yourself
to the size of a child to get through,
    like threading yourself through
the eye of a needle.
    There is immediate entry at this
tiny, unsung gate;
    no crowds are eagerly queuing up
        to rush in.
    You may be quite alone
for most of your journey,
    but I promise you,
when you have finished the course,
    fought the good fight,
        struggled with opposition,
and broken through from without and from within,
    you will come upon a heavenly throng
    with their voices resounding in cheers.
My Son stands in the midst of them,
    His arms outstretched toward you,
        welcoming you Home.

>   Oh,
> Beloved, I live at the narrow gate,
>> and the cross of Calvary is the narrow road.
> The way is lonely and filled with hardship, but
>> at its end
>>> you walk in My soul.

Luke 13:24; Proverbs 16:25; Romans 8:7; 5:18; 1
Timothy 5:6; Luke 12:19; Matthew 16:24–25; Psalm
73:24; John 12:26

The Gift of Gentleness

Thou hast also given me the shield of thy salvation; and thy gentleness hath made me great.

(2 Sam. 22:36)

At times your need for the approval of people
    can be greater
than your desire to please Me.
    Then you become frustrated and
lose your sweetness of temper.
    Your heart forms a crust,
and you cannot be easily won back to Me.

At these times you are especially
    hard on yourself.
Your longing for love and acceptance
    outweighs the loveliness
I have formed in you;
    and your kind heart,

which cherishes and holds dear the needs of others,
  becomes a gathering place for pain and despair.

When you are needy and hungry
  and you long for satisfying companionship,
be gentle on yourself.
  Do not despise your longing heart.
Do not consider your own pain as trivial.
  How can you behave with a suave manner,
be conciliatory, fair and patient to others
  when you are not gentle on yourself?
Allow holy gentleness to minister to you;
  permit yourself to be comforted and encouraged
by My gentle thoughts,
  by My love.
  I am never threatening, nasty, alienating, or
unkind to you.
  The judging, spiteful, competitive hurdles
you must leap in life
  require My gentleness to guide you.

Today,
be gentle to yourself.

Psalm 18:35; 2 Corinthians 10:1; Romans 8:1; 1
Thessalonians 2:7

The Gift of Fairness

The Lord in the midst of her is
[uncompromisingly] righteous; He will not
do iniquity; every morning He brings His
justice to light, He fails not.

(Zeph. 3:5)

Keep before you the image of truth,
    though iniquity and injustice
surround you as angry, roaring lions
    and faith is attacked by wolves.
Do not cringe before officials and judges
    who gnaw on the bones of the innocent,
and false prophets and priests who profane the
sanctuary.
    There will always be white dragons in your midst
        preaching their own word
            pretending it is Mine,
but if you keep the Truth before your face,
    hard as brass, immovable as steel,

156

you will not be shaken.

I am fair and just.
    I rest with satisfaction
    in My love for My children,
those who walk in integrity.
I exult and become joyful
    and My song spreads over them
like a blanket.
    They shall hear Me forever,
        for they have fallen in love
with the sound of My voice.
    The sins of the world and the injustice
done to them cannot turn their ears
    from My voice.

See! Even as My beloved ones are
    unjustly imprisoned, they lift up their voices
and sing the songs they hear in their hearts.
    (My sheep hear My voice!)
It is not the world's injustice
    that you should fear,
        but the perfect justice of the Lord.
    The holy outstretched hand of God
        is more powerful
        than the wrinkled fist of the world.

I am always just and fair. I recompense evil for evil.

Righteousness and justice are the foundation
    of My throne.
The whole earth will know it,
    so be glad, My dear one.
I know thy works and I have set before you
    an open door:
        No person can shut it.
If it is fairness and justice you seek,
    look not to the world,
but to Me.

    Then, be still,
    and listen.

Zephaniah 3:3–5, 17; Acts 16:25; Psalm 97:2, 6;
Revelation 3:8; Psalm 46:10

The Gift of Conscience

*And Paul, looking intently at the Council,
said, "Brethren, I have lived my life with a
perfectly good conscience before God up to
this day."*

(Acts 23:1)

Do your best always to maintain
a blameless conscience
    before Me
    and before people.
Your conscience is a gift to be used
    for inner awareness,
to help you see completely
    and to understand
and be informed,
        morally.
I want your conscience
    void of offense—
clear, unshaken

and blameless,
both in the sight of people
and Me.

Do not be misled;
keep on good terms with your conscience
and give no energy to thoughts or opinions
that are contrary to Me.
There are some whose consciences are weak.
These little ones are uncertain,
like newborn colts on wobbly legs.
They are unstable and untrained
by the Master's love and wisdom.
I do not expect of them
the same that I expect of a disciple
whose conscience is exercised and in use.
And so, My dear one,
do not seek your own good,
advantage and profit,
but seek the welfare of others.
Then your conscience will testify
of your devout and pure motives,
your godly sincerity
and your avoidance of fleshly wisdom.
You will recognize pride as a poisonous serpent;
you will call envy by its name;
you will shun greed and unholy anger;
you will be no friend of sloth or gluttony;

and lust will not camp on your doorstep,
>not for a moment.
Let your conscience be your witness.
I want your loving interest in the world
>around you
to spring from a pure heart,
>from a clear conscience
and from your sincere, unfeigned faith.
>So hold fast to your faith
>>and lean your entire human personality
>>on Me
>in absolute trust and confidence.
Then you will develop a clear and holy conscience.

>The ungodly do not have this illuminated,
secret gift shining from their inner person.
>They must depend upon human ethics and values,
>>unkissed by My Holy Spirit.
>It is their sorrow and shame,
for their joy of life becomes twisted
>and wrung dry so easily.
Ah, but the person who walks uprightly,
>living a noble life, behaving honorably,
completely honest in all things
>with a clear conscience—
this one's joy cannot be twisted,
>nor can it be wrung dry.

Today,
will you examine and clean your conscience?

Acts 24:16; 1 Corinthians 8:7; 10:24; 2 Corinthians 1:12;
Romans 2:15; 1 Timothy 1:5, 19; 3:9; Hebrews 13:18

The Gift of Brokenness

The sacrifices of God are a broken spirit; A broken and a contrite heart, O God, Thou wilt not despise.

(Ps. 51:17)

I love those who love Me,
and I am a shield to those who walk
    in integrity.
I guard the paths of justice
    and I preserve the way of the godly.

I keep My promises.
    I will seek the lost
who cry for My help.
    I will bring back the scattered,
and I will bandage the wounded
    and the crippled.
I will strengthen the weak and the sick,
    and I will caress the broken bones.

I am near to the hurting heart,
    and I save those whose sins
crush them with remorse.
    I hear the prayers of the humble,
and I respond to the pleading
    of the thoroughly penitent.
I will destroy the hardhearted
    and perverse;
I will feed them with judgment and punishment,
    for I hate a proud and arrogant heart.
For I observe the one who struts through mountains of
music,
    rings and jewels glittering,
        white clothing shining,
    bearing Jesus banners
and religious trinkets
    and I shake My head,
        do I know this one?
                              So, in the light of My
words,
    which reflect the light of My will,
tell me:
Why do you boast?

Proverbs 8:17; 2:8; Ezekiel 34:16a; Psalm 34:18; 101:5;
Ezekiel 34:16b; Matthew 7:22–23

The Gift of the Yoke

Take My yoke upon you, and learn from
Me, for I am gentle and humble in heart;
and you shall find rest for your souls.
(Matt. 11:29)

When your emotions are like positioned killers
ready to attack,
    and when the turmoil of your mind
is worse than a hundred hurricanes,
    and your heart feels crumpled and shredded
like old papers to throw out,
    I am here, My love, for you.
Right here for you.

Come now, let Me hold you.
Let Me kiss you;
    you are safe with Me.
I am here beside you,
    yoked with you—

you and I together.

I have not left you helpless
to battle the hounds of hell alone,
   nor have I left you
to battle yourself alone.

   Hush now as My gentle heart
refreshes your burdened heart.

   Pause and allow
the blessed quiet of My mind,
   to bring quiet to your mind
for it is *My* yoke you are bound to.

   The effects of righteousness
are peace without and within,
   and the results of righteousness
are quietness and confident trust forever.

   I will never hurt you
nor afflict you, My beloved child.

   I remove the mental labor
and the agony you suffer
   to give you rest.

      I relieve and refresh your soul.
Oh, learn of Me and listen.

   How can you hear Me beside you
when you're yanking at the yoke?

   If you would observe the jeweled yoke
we wear on our necks,

perhaps your crown would not seem so heavy.
We are bound together,
    you and I—
yoked,
    like two oxen pulling a cart.
But sometimes you seem to forget
    My gentle, meek and lowly heart
allows Me to do the pulling,
    not you.

Matthew 11:28–30; Isaiah 32:17

The Gift of the Burden

For my yoke is easy, and my burden is light.

(Matt. 11:30)

When you are in distress,
you must call to me;
    I will answer.
    If you bear the cares of your heart
on your shoulders,
    the heaviness will buckle your knees
and stiffen your neck.
    I relieve you of the burden.

Your hands become cold, unbending, sore,
as you labor painfully to carry others' troubles
    like large baskets of bricks.
        I free your hands.

In the secret thunder

      of your fears,
I come to you
    and I offer you the privilege
of casting your burdens on Me.
Release the weight,
and see if I will sustain you.

    You fret over the sins of others
when your own sins
    wash over your head
like waves of a flood,
      too heavy to lift.
    Resentment, anger, bitterness,
are heavy burdens:
    They exile you from love
and eat your bones.
    You become a reproach to yourself;
you wax weary, heavily burdened
    and creaking with hurts.

I give you a new burden,
    sweet and beautiful,
to keep yourself from evil.
It is no more difficult than the one
    you carry now
(which brings me no pleasure).

    Now give me your old burden

and I will give you Mine.

New and sweet

light

and easy.

Psalm 81:6; 55:22; 38:4; Zephaniah 3:18; Job 7:20; Acts
15:28–29

The Gift of Tears

Mine eye poureth out tears unto God.
(Job 16:20)

Do you dine on tears
    day and night,
because you weep with those who weep,
    My crying child?
Are your tears, which build high towers
    like tidal waves,
for the sins of others?
    Or do your tears water your pillow,
because of your penitent heart and
    do you weep in shame and sorrow
for your own sins?
Or do you pour out your thirsting soul,
    panting and hungry for Me
because the world shouts,
    "Where is your God?"
Tell Me why your soul despairs.

Oh is that joy I see,
glistening tears of ecstasy?
The tears of laughter and rejoicing
refresh the soul;
they warm the eyelids and the cheeks
and replenish the fountains of your mind.

Love, I will be gracious to you,
I will blot out your transgressions
and wash you thoroughly from your sin.
Against Me and Me only,
do the children of humankind sin.
But I desire truth in your innermost being
and Wisdom to be master of your thoughts.
Your tears may not always be the result
of the truth;
tears may not always be born of Wisdom.
And so I tell you,
I will wipe the tears of travail and pain
away from your face, which is dear to Me.

My Son shall guide you to
relief,
forgiveness, assurance and
to the springs of the water of life.
There, I will wipe away every stain.

When you sow in tears,

you will reap in joyful singing.
The grief and sorrows of today
    will not last,
for I comfort you
    in My embrace
and give to you the gift of tears,
    which I keep in bottles on My holy shelf.
    Nothing pertaining to you
escapes My gaze.
    When you cry, dear one,
give your tears to Me,
    where they are safe.

Psalm 6:6; 42:1–4; 51:1–4a, 6; Isaiah 25:8; Revelation
7:11; Psalm 126:5

The Gift of Satisfaction

And I will fill the soul of the priests with abundance, And My people shall be satisfied with My goodness, declares the Lord.

(Jer. 31:14)

It may seem to you
    that satisfaction
is not attainable in your lifetime.
    You may conclude with dread
that the pressing cares of life
    are far too weighty,
too morbidly oppressive
    and polluted
for joy to burrow through.
    You behave like a scarecrow
in a field of cucumbers,
    a reproach and a tattered messenger,
a false advertisement.

You announce to others that there is no hope,
because there is no one to rescue you
　　from your sins of self-concern
and self-pity.

　　But life is bigger than your personal world,
and I am telling you today
　　that I am here to satisfy your soul.
Even in the driest, most selfish drought,
　　I am here to satisfy your mouth,
your taste buds and your vocabulary
　　with good things,
because I am your unfailing source
　　of total satisfaction.
Lack of satisfaction
　　is a gift from My hand, too,
for only in your dissatisfaction
　　will you seek Me early,
will you cry out for My help,
　　and hear Me when I answer.

I want to remove the yoke of heaviness
　　from your midst.
Stop pointing your finger
　　and speaking wickedness.
Leave vanity behind you,
　　and stretch your arms to Me for forgiveness
and renewal of your mind.

Learn to give true concern and care
to those in need
    so you will hear Me when I tell you
to feed those who are hungry
    and assist those
who suffer mental and physical affliction.

Then watch as your glory rises in darkness
and your gloom is transformed into
    bright, noon-sun candescence.
You shall live in a house of love, and
    I shall continually guide you.
I satisfy your soul.

Do not be so quick to accept the pitiable life of a
scarecrow.
It is not My plan for you
    to live out your days
hanging from a stick in the sun.
    Even wounded birds fly from
arms that have no flesh.
    I want to help you out
of such a helpless state.
    When your soul thirsts,
allow Me the honor
    of satisfying that thirst

and give Me the privilege
of giving wings to a heart
that longs to fly.

Isaiah 1:8; 58:10–11; Psalm 103:3; 107:6, 9

The Gift of Trust

The Lord is good, a strong hold in the day
of trouble; and he knoweth them that trust
in him.

(Nah. 1:7)

I know those
whose desire is fixed on favors
and hoped-for blessings,
and I know those whose
desire to trust
is greater than the desire
for answered prayer.

Do not confuse trust
with your intensely felt *wants*.
Your wants are not trust.
Your needs are not trust.
Your hopes are not trust.
Anxious appeals are not trust.

I have said to trust Me at *all times,*

    because I am a refuge;

    I am a shield;

    I am Help;

    there is safety and rest

in releasing your many worries to Me.

    I have told you

to trust Me

    and safely snuggle, like a young bird

beneath the shadow

    of its mother's mighty wings,

not just for special favors,

    a worm, an insect,

or a miracle here and there.

    Trust Me to be *Me.*

If you trust Me as I ask you to,

    you may then begin to understand

(and even love)

    the infinite wisdom and compassion

when I answer with a holy no

    to your requests.

There is a purpose for the lions and the beasts;

    only through My eyes can you see and

understand.

    Trust removes the rumbling mist of fear,

and it will be settled in your mind forever

    that your life,

your work,

your loves,
your health,
your prayers,
your past,
your future
   are in My mercy.

You are soldered into the center of My eye.
   Trust Me.

Psalm 62:8; 115:9–11; 36:7, 9; 32:10; Matthew 6:20;
Deuteronomy 3:10; Psalm 17:8

The Gift of
Memory

Thus saith the Lord; I remember thee.

(Jer. 2:2)

I have inscribed you on the palms of My hands;
I will never forget you.
My promises to you are imprinted in My heart,
because My love for you
surpasses time and generations.

As the rainbow reminds the earth of my solemn
pledge
to hold back the flood waters
from ever again swallowing all that lives,
so will I remind you.
As you walk through the cities of the world,
which are like furnaces of smoke
and consuming islands of fire,
you, My righteous one,

are fixed indelibly on My mind,
never to be erased.

Nothing befalls you that I am not aware of.
When your soul faints within you,
remember Me,
and remember that I will save you
from all that terrifies you.
Remember the marvelous deeds I have done
and that I am Lord of all there is.
(This is why you have a memory.)
Remember that you are mine
and My tender mercies surround you.
Even your dreams are precious to Me
when you share them with Me.
I remember that you are a human being,
dust,
and your life is short;
and you must remember
that I am the God of eternity and all creation.
I will be Lord of your memory;
and you will remember and think on good,
not evil,
you will remember My works
and My love.
For day and night My Holy Spirit
increases your memory,

heightens your awareness
    and reminds you of all
I have said to you.

    Your memory is a gift from Me
as a reflection of My own.

Isaiah 49:16; Psalm 105:8; Genesis 19:29; Jonah 2:7;
Psalm 106:10; 103:14; 89:47; John 14:26

The Gift of
Purity

*And every one who has this hope fixed on
Him [Jesus] purifies himself, just as He is
pure.*

(1 John 3:3)

I have already purified your heart
    by a holy work of My Spirit,
and yet I call you to an even purer walk
    than the one you walk today.
I call you
    to higher provinces of faith,
where your spirit will soar unhindered
    and where your soul mounts up to ride
upon the integrity of My holiness.

Leave the dark, cloudless nights
of sin and temptation
    far beneath you.
I call you to upper regions,

higher,
higher.

I call you to see Me, to know Me
    with a higher perception,
one that is nobler, purer,
    fired by upward holy passion,
to separate you
    from the din of everyday
goodwill and common courtesy.
    You are more than good.
    You are more than kind.
    You are more than a decent person.
You are empowered by My Spirit to
    be holy as I am holy,
    as My Son is holy,
    as My Spirit is holy.

So *up*! My beloved,
    separate your thoughts
and set your mind apart
    from your fears.
Prepare yourself for the upward climb;
    prepare to fly!
There is no higher place
    in heaven or on earth
than the blessed altitude
    where only the pure in heart can soar.

I have said the pure in heart are blessed,

    those who pray from higher ground and

brush the cheek of God.

    They shall see Me.

1 Peter 1:16; Psalm 99:3; Hebrews 7:26; Luke 11:13;
Joshua 7:13; 8:1; Matthew 5:8

The Gift of Silence

But the Lord is in His holy temple; let all
the earth hush and keep silence before Him.
(Hab. 2:20)

Are you afraid of stillness?
Does quietness alarm you—
remind you of your aloneness?

Perhaps that is why
your life tends to be so noisy,
and you think yourself
brash, boorish,
like a thrashing mule at times,
or like a prating ox.

I want you to be silent before Me.
I want you to listen diligently
to the quiet.
Be still.

Hush.

Know that I am God.

Can you pierce the heavens
with your noise?

Can you trample your way into My eyes
with your pleas and promises?

I have seen you.
I have known you
without a sound.
My silence is perfect communication
issuing from My holiness.
It is My sigh of love,
My bond with you
through My written Word
and My Spirit.
You were formed as
the final work of My creation,
an act I performed
in silence
with a breath.
You are My sigh,
My heart,
My breath.

Will you not hush,
still your pride,
and stop your racing thoughts?

Will you cease from involving yourself
in matters that do not pertain to you
    and problems too great for you?
Hush! Compose and quiet your mind.
    Let your soul rest as a weaned baby rests
against the quiet circumference
    of a mother's body.
Listen to the stillness,
    where no calamity can reach,
    where human plans cannot rule,
    where the needy personality is
        lifted from the ash heap
            as if on wings of a dove
            to a holy place
    away from the stormy winds of daily cares
    and the continual flux of human motion.

Enter into yourself
    and listen to the stillness of
My life
    deep,
        deep,
deep in you.

Psalm 46:10; Zechariah 2:13; Zephaniah 1:7; Psalm
131:1–2; 113:7

The Gift of Simplicity

But I am afraid, lest as the serpent deceived
Eve by his craftiness, your minds should be
led astray from the simplicity and purity of
devotion to Christ.

(2 Cor. 11:3)

I reside at the center of your being,
   where there is no fragmentation.
I transcend both fear and human reason.

   I am the core and substance of life,
where there is no success or failure.

   I illuminate the earth and all that is in it,
and you have the personality of this light.

   You have within you the kernel
of divine self-acceptance,
      needful to resist the urge to rush along
with the human stampede

who wildly chase after attention, riches,
possessions,
and the current cultural pursuit,
    be it winning a battle with hand-hewn spears
or painting the rumps of ponies,
    it is not without guile.
The silly and seducible
    pursue the concerns of the flesh,
but the innocent doves of God
    pursue the higher things of God.

My Son came to you holy,
    innocent, undefiled,
        unstained by sin,
and it is His cross you carry,
    His life you lead,
        His words you live by.
Seek My kingdom first,
    and you shall have
all that your heart has longed for.
    Simplicity discerns what is evil
with a single eye,
    and in the joyful sweetness of your wisdom,
you will choose only what glorifies your God.

    Your only possessions

are what your soul can part with.

    In simplicity
    you are truly free.

Hebrews 7:26; Matthew 10:16; 6:25, 33

The Gift of
Kindness

*For the mountains shall depart, and the
hills be removed; but my kindness shall not
depart from thee.*

(Isa. 54:10)

How often is kindness thought of
merely as good breeding?
an act of good manners?
"How kind of you,"
you tell the grocer,
or the person at the ticket counter.
I hear you. I hear the words.
Like the word "love" you fling around.

Did you ever stop to ponder
if I love chocolate,
or shiny cars,
or rainy days,
or nights by the fire,

or walks on the beach?
   I do not love these things.
I love *you*.
   And kindness is intimately expressive
of love.

   Kindness originates in the heart of heaven,
deep in the mind of God.
   For it is My kindness that keeps you
tightly fastened to My right side,
   where you cannot be removed,
no, not by disintegrating mountains
   or by hills that convulse,
and not even by the foul breath of your sins.
   My kindness sent you a Savior
to forgive you
   of every unrighteous, nasty move you make,
every unclean storm you blow across the valleys of
   your own life
and the lives of others.

   If you could only see the pain you serve
like cakes of salt,
   if you could count the jars of tears
you have provoked,
   if you could stand with Me and watch
small, young shoulders trembling on the bed,
   sobs muffled by a wet pillow,

little hands clenched in defeat.

    It is not a mighty conqueror
who steals a child's contentment—
oh, if you knew,
    if you understood!

If you considered your salvation seriously,
    you would leap across your life
        with gratitude and joy.
You would gladly wear
    the coat of kindness.
My dear, I am kind to you,
    because I love you.
I forgive you,
    because I love you.
I am tenderhearted, full of mercy.
    I am kind.

    Now you be as I am.

Ephesians 4:32; Titus 3:4

The Gift of Ministry

Now I know that the Lord saves His
anointed; He will answer from His holy
heaven, with the saving strength of His
right hand.

(Ps. 20:6)

I call you, as a little gray bird,
   to move about the earth on spidery legs,
with a voice as soft as the sound of the dew,
   quite defenseless,
weighing less than a hiccough.

But all around you are troops
of drooling, ravening wolves,
   ready to devour anything at all,
      anyone at all,
         especially tiny, helpless birds.
   The speeding feet of enemy wolves
thunder in the dirt;

their voices howl,
they are wild with hunger.
They are mad, insane.
They hate your song.
They cannot fly.

And you, My little bird,
are called to loose the bonds of wickedness
these wolves promote as normal living.
I call to you, "Undo the chains!
Set the oppressed free."
The wolves have chewed, devoured, held captive,
made homeless, stripped and starved My people.
And My people have allowed it.
They sigh, "That's life."
But then they raise their voices like trumpets,
and they screech for help in the night.
Whom shall I send, My little gray dove?
I send you.

You go into all the world and tell them
of the higher places to soar;
sing them My new song;
bring the light to the darkness.
Because you ride on the heights,
your wings have become like those of an eagle,
yet you will not boast of the strength
of chariots or horses.

You can soar above the clouds
     as a flame of fire.
Never lose heart!
     I give you the words,
     the strength, the anointing;
the Gift.
     Soar with Me.

Isaiah 58; Matthew 10:16; 28:18–20; Psalm 20:7; 104:4;
Galatians 6:9; Isaiah 59:21

The Gift of Hope

For in hope we have been saved, but hope that is
seen is not hope; for why does one also hope for
what he sees? But if we hope for what we do not
see, with perseverance we wait eagerly for it.
(Rom. 8:24–25)

I understand, My child,
when you are uncertain about My will,
 when you cry out
in the lonely moments of your despair
 for the life of a loved one,
for physical healing,
 healing of relationships
that have gone awry like sprung coils;
 Dear one, do not lose heart,
do not lose hope.

 I am Hope.
I give you more than future glory,
 I am your *present* glory.

I do hear you;
    I do answer you.

My ears are not closed to your requests
    and your fervent prayers,
but you must have hope. Trust Me!
    I know your heart, I hear you,
but My will cannot be flopped like a fish on the sand.
    I cannot change
because you fast, or plead,
    or because you insist you know more than I.

Allow My written Word,
    which throbs with the power of hope,
to enter your mind and body
    like fresh blood in your veins,
new life in your thoughts.

    Your hope of glory is in My Son,
the One who works on building your mansion
    daily.
But how will you love His holy hammer
    without the hope of eternal life
that I promised ages ago
    (and I cannot lie)?
And how will you be recognized
    if you are not wearing your helmet
of hope?

And how will your soul relax
in the trials of life
    if you do not perceive in the far reaches
of your mind
that I give you more
    than miracles?

When you have My mind,
    My wisdom,
My knowledge,
    My understanding,
you will not panic
    at the threat of death.
Instead, you will march through it
    as if it were only a valley,
because I am with you.
Do not be afraid, My child.
    Caress the sister of love,
    which is My gift of hope,
and bravely
    come through
        the darkness.

Romans 15:4; Colossians 1:27: John 14:2, 6; Colossians
1:23; 1:5; Romans 5:2; 1 Thessalonians 5:8; Titus 1:2;
Psalm 23:4

The Gift of Safety

For Thou hast been a refuge for me, a tower
of strength against the enemy. Let me dwell
in Thy tent forever; Let me take refuge in
the shelter of Thy wings.

(Ps. 61:3–4)

Trust in My Name,
  in My power to deliver you
  from the peril of death
and the dread of evil.

It is written upon the tablet of your heart,
  by My perfect Holy Spirit,
that I never fail
  to honor the trust and confidence of My children
  who know Me for Who I Am
and are certain in their trust.
  Answered prayer is not to be collected
like hobby items

to be displayed at religious carnivals.
The child of God
knows I always answer,
and he is content even if I do not
give what is requested of Me.

Trust Me
and you will not be afraid
of the task ahead of you.
Trust Me
and you will not slip,
slide or stumble.
Trust Me
and you will not be desolate.
Trust Me
and you will know you are safe
even when it appears
you are not.
Trust Me
and you will be
My friend.

2 Corinthians 1:10; Proverbs 1:33; Psalm 31:1; 56:11;
Jeremiah 31:9; Psalm 34:22; Matthew 7:7; James 2:23

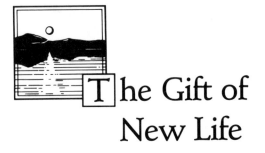

The Gift of New Life

*And just as we have borne the image of the
earthy, we shall also bear the image of the
heavenly.*

(1 Cor. 15:49)

Never think it odd or terrible
    if your prayers seem to go unanswered,
or your long vigil of pain seems unending.
I want your heart full of My grace,
    I want to be known in you,
not by your suffering,
    but through your victory.

As your passion to protect yourself
    diminishes,
you will hear Me more clearly.
    As your drive to earn approval decreases,
you will appreciate My approval more.
    As you cast your financial worries

at the foot of the cross,
   you become freer, healthier, clearer of mind.
As your hope for earthly security
   is abandoned,
you will be more confident in heaven's care.
   As your own strength and abilities
are exchanged for Mine,
   you become strong and able
and an instrument for My strength and ability.
   As your efforts to be physically fit
are given to Me
   and I am permitted to become your personal
trainer,
your temple will no longer be a curse to you.
   As your burning fervor for learning
is wholly given to Me,
   you become a wiser and a more intrepid scholar.
(You are a student of the Master Teacher!)
   As your burning drive to be cherished
by another person is relinquished,
   you can concentrate better
on capturing My heart.
   As your fear of growing old vanishes,
you will become flooded with new energy and vision.
   As ministry cares are put into My hands,
your own hands are free to better help others.
   As you lose your fear of death,
you are free to live your life

with enthusiasm
    and joy.

Then you can focus
    on becoming more beautifully
like Me.

The Gift of Turning

"Yet even now," declares the Lord, "return
to Me with all your heart."

(Joel 2:12a)

Where is the happy countenance of My beloved?
Is that mud on your chin?
    Blood?
        Why do you weep?
Who has taught you to grapple with temptation
        on your own?
    Who has instructed you
in the ways of wrath and
    a winking eye?

I have put a lamp within you
    to search the spirit,
        the spirit of your inmost being;
it is the place where you have known

and appreciated My lavish gifts
of divine favor and blessing.
I have not guided you by human wisdom,
but I have taught you by the Holy Spirit,
for human wisdom
does not accept or welcome Me.
No one knows the thoughts of God
except the Spirit of God.

You have not received the spirit of the world,
and that is why you bleed.

Turn and I will bathe your wounds
in My healing love and mercy.
I will multiply My abundant pardon
and change your mourning to joy;
for though you try to bulldoze mountains
to level them in rubble and destruction,
and though you shake with fury the hilly terrain
of your life,
My love and kindness hold you tenderly,
to My heart,
and I shall always be your God of peace.
I love you.

Return to Me.

Proverbs 20:27; 16:30a; 1 Corinthians 2:11–14; Psalm
7:15–16; Isaiah 55:7; Jeremiah 31:13; Isaiah 54:10